"Life's a funny thing.
Nobody wants to get old,
but they don't want to die
young, either."

-KEITH RICHARDS[1]

1 *Keith Richards: Under the Influence* (US: 2015), dir. Morgan Neville, prod. Tremolo Productions/Radical Media, dist. Netflix, 81 mins.

SIMMONS BOOKS

GENE SIMMONS

WITHDRAWN

27

THE LEGEND & MYTHOLOGY OF THE 27 CLUB

GENE SIMMONS 27

pH

powerHouse Books Brooklyn, NY

Robert Johnson (1911-1938) Brian Jones (1942-1969) Jimi Hendrix (1942-1970) Janis Joplin (1943-1970) Jim Morrison (1943-1971) Jean-Michel Basquiat (1960-1988) Kurt Cobain (1967-1994) Amy Winehouse (1983-2011) Alan "Blind Owl" Wilson (1943-1970) Ron "Pigpen" McKernan (1945-1973) Jonathan Brandis (1976-2003) Otis Redding (1941-1967) Tim Buckley (1947-1975) Jeff Buckley (1966-1997)

Introduction 10

27

Robert Johnson (1938) 34
Brian Jones (1969) 50
Jimi Hendrix (1970) 64
Janis Joplin (1970) 84
Jim Morrison (1971) 104
Jean-Michel Basquiat (1988) 124
Kurt Cobain (1994) 146
Amy Winehouse (2011) 172

Notable Mentions 194
Alan "Blind Owl" Wilson (1970) 200
Ron "Pigpen" McKernan (1973) 206
Jonathan Brandis (2003) 212

The Almost-27s 218
Otis Redding (1967) 220
Tim Buckley (1975) and Jeff Buckley (1997) 228

The Science of 27 238
Final Thoughts: Avicii, and the Future 252
Acknowledgments 261
Index 262

This book is dedicated to everyone
whose lives have been affected by
mental illness, addiction, or both,
especially the young musicians out
there who struggle but who still dream
of picking up a guitar, sitting down at a
keyboard, or picking up a microphone.
Keep going.

Introduction

"Revisiting these memories again and again (and we do) can feel traumatic, and the most sensational details still shock decades later. But there's a more expansive, alternate history component at work, too, imagining what these legends might have created had they lived, and how their absence has shaped the music and popular culture that followed."[2]

2   "Celebrity Deaths That Changed Music History: Gone Too Soon," by David Browne, RollingStone.com, 08/14/2017.

Introduction

It is the year 2018, and we are losing legends like leaves in autumn. The end of my era, and the era that inspired my era, is on its way. McCartney and the Stones chug away with gusto, but there is no denying the waning of a certain creative golden era in pop culture. There will be a time when all the icons of a certain kind, finally, are gone. In the past two years alone, we've lost David Bowie, Prince, Tom Petty, Glenn Fry, my dear friend Hugh Hefner, Harry Dean Stanton, Chris Cornell...the list goes on, and trying to be exhaustive makes leaving out someone important an inevitability.

When they leave us, we tend to make saints of them or, at the very least, romanticize them. Death puts us all in a reflective and revisionist mood, and we polish, if not actively rewrite, the histories of our heroes.

We build them up or tear them down, and construct narratives around their passing that make sense to us. At times, it is justified; at other times, we are biased and our emotions get the better of us.

Why so many, now? Why all at once, so close together, barely giving us time to take a breath and grieve before the next? Looking for patterns is simply what we, as humans, do. We are pattern-seeking animals, and it is in our nature to make sense of things that throw our lives out of order.

By my lights, the reason (if there really is just one reason) that so many are dying now is because there was a magical period of time when pop cultural *Legends*, with a capital "L," were born, all very close to one another. A special kind of figure—a timeless figure, from a unique era; it is only natural that they should all reach their twilight years at around the same time as well. The generational wheel turns and takes entire cultural movements with it. It stands to reason that there is one generation, one chunk of time, that was uniquely influential, because we notice all of our legends die at once when it comes to pass. Narrowly, I judge this magic time as the early-60s to the late-70s, but there are notable exceptions outside of those sand-drawn lines, as there are to every rule. Elvis is one exception.

Our obsession with celebrity death is only exceeded, it seems, by our obsession with *young* celebrity death. When cultural figures pass in their twilight years, we can process it as somehow comprehensible, although sad. Our reflection on their careers is appropriately calm—less frenzied and conspiratorial. However, when a figure seems to pass in their greatest strides, at the peak of our expectations for them, we tend to obsess, and even aggrandize it as somehow exciting or mythical. We invent conspiracy theories. We are shell-shocked, confused, fascinated. We analyze, review, replay again and again. Perhaps this is all simply our way of trying to make sense of senseless things.

After 1969, a slew of major musicians all died in quick succession. Brian Jones (founding member of the Rolling Stones), Janis Joplin, Jimi Hendrix, and Jim Morrison of the Doors, arguably the biggest rock stars of their time, all passed at 27 years of age, within just three years of each other.

Whether this was coincidence, simply a logical result of their lifestyle choices, drugs or mental illness, the pressures of being a public figure, or some combination of all of these factors combined, people began to notice a pattern. Correlation began to equal causation in the public imagination. An urban myth, and subsequent cultural fixation, was born: the "27 club."

As the idea gained traction, pre-1960s figures such as Robert Johnson (one of the, if not *the*, most influential bluesmen of all time), also dead at 27, were included, as well as post-1980s figures such as Kurt Cobain and Amy Winehouse. The true origin of the word "club" in the term "27 club" is unknown, and there are a few different theories thrown around about who said it first.

For most people, the question nags: why 27 *specifically*? What is so unique and deadly about that number? Why so many, why the *most* famous, the *most* revered? Was there some sort of curse, some sort of reason for it all? An idea—that there were more deaths of famous musicians and cultural figures at 27 than at any other age—took form, spread, and conspiracies began to formulate.

Now, this supposed "statistical spike" of musicians dying at 27 is not quite true—as it happens, almost as many famous musicians die at 25, or 32.[3] A study, done by the peer-reviewed *British Medical Journal*, concluded the following: "We identified three deaths at age 27 amongst 522 musicians at risk, giving a rate of 0.57 deaths per 100 musician years. Similar death rates were observed at ages 25 (rate=0.56) and 32 (0.54). There was no peak in risk around age 27."[4]

But, since when has hard science ever dissuaded the mob or the media? A cultural obsession was taking form, an urban myth was spreading, and it bled across the years into the 90s. As it is with many conspiracies and urban legends, this one contained a kernel of truth: fame and youth *can* be a destructive combination. Though the number 27 does not appear to be significant, youth and fame more generally *is* statistically different. The study found that, "the risk of death for famous musicians throughout their 20s and 30s was *two to three times higher*

3   "Does the 27 club exist?" by M. Wolkewitz, A. Allignol, N. Graves, AG Barnett. *The BMJ*, Vol. 343, 12/2011.
4   Ibid.

than the general UK population." [5]

The 27 club, then, can be viewed as symbolic of this trend, even if age 27 is not, in fact, its sole peak.

When writing a book about this sort of topic, being sensitive, while still being brave enough not to shy away from the facts, is important. Needless to say, being sensitive has not always been my strong suit, but I'll try. While fans naturally deify their heroes, these figures were people of flesh and blood, like the rest of us, and many of them are survived by loved ones who do not view their demise as romantic—and who loathe the constant speculation, tabloid attention, and conspiracy theories that fans bombard them with daily.

The concept of the 27 club, in my view, should not be about how glamorous it is to die young—at the peak of success, in a flurry of drugs and excess. This is the way it is usually described, and I've been vocal about disapproving of this line of thinking. Even those who, themselves, participate in drug-use and excess are not necessarily on board with its glamorization; Kurt Cobain himself, to his credit, said in an interview, "I never went out of my way to say anything about my drug use [...] I think people who glamorize drugs are fucking assholes, and if there's a hell, they'll go there." [6] I tend to agree. To the families and friends of these people, and of people all around the world who met similar fates at the hands of

---

5   Ibid.
6   "Dark Side of the Womb: Part 2," by the Stud Brothers, *Melody Maker*, 08/28/1993.

that deadly cocktail of drug use and mental illness, there is nothing glamorous or heroic about losing someone you love, or losing your own life.

However, what I did not realize in my (slightly) younger years is that the story can neither be about scolding the figures themselves for their choices, which is what I have been known to do, publicly and relentlessly, in the past. One especially cannot truly understand another's experience if, like me, they have never taken drugs themselves. That place, after someone is already addicted to drugs, is a place I've never been. Similarly, this crazy public life we (the famous and infamous) find ourselves in is difficult to describe to those who have never experienced it. I have nothing to complain about—I live my dream every day. But make no mistake: fame and infamy are strange things, and people find themselves there through hard work, creativity, and luck, but it can still be a bewildering and disturbing experience. It can change your personality, blind you in many ways, and alter your perception of the world around you in unpredictable ways. I can attest to this blindness myself; when you stand in front of thousands of people screaming your name, you become a little like Lawrence of Arabia, believing your own legend, feeling invincible to harm.

The phrase itself, 27 *club*, is problematic in my view (take it from me; the king of saying tone-deaf things in public). I've seen articles, and even heard industry people mention it the same way they might talk about Soho House: a private, exclusive, members-only "club."

(Incidentally, it is interesting to note that the fee for a Soho House membership is less expensive for those under 27, and more for those older than 27, specifically, as if turning 27 is a coming-of-age for the creative class. I am not sure if this is a deliberate allusion, but it sure seems convenient.)

It's easy to forget we're talking about actual death when this is the agreed upon jargon, a value system weighted so thoroughly toward youth that has been in place so long we barely even notice. To state it plainly: death should not be a club. Yet, if you look up these figures online, you see them grouped together. There are fan-run websites that sell unlicensed merch and t-shirts with these people assembled like a pantheon of gods, sometimes with phrases like "forever 27" adorned on them, along with stylized Grim Reapers. Somehow, these merchandisers are excused from the moral outrage that they, perhaps, would have had directed at them had these young people's deaths not occurred under the guise of being "rock stars." [7]

If anything, learning about the 27 club should be about learning about why people do what they do; you can never truly get inside someone's head, but making one's best effort to get as close as possible is the key, I believe, to every kind of diplomacy. But, as I've said, diplomacy was never my strong suit. So, this book is my attempt.

Sure, it can be a cautionary tale of the perils and

---

7   "About Us," Forever27.co.uk, accessed: 06/11/2018.

pitfalls that come with undiagnosed mental health issues, as well as how those issues are magnified and inflamed by an industry and a culture that glorifies dangerous behavior. It can be a story about how pop culture convinces people (when they are too young to know better) that they are invincible, and, simultaneously and paradoxically, that death is preferable to old age. "I hope I die before I get old," sing The Who. "What a drag it is getting old," sing the Stones. These sentiments have been with us a long time, and they are, unfortunately, still a big part of pop culture mythos; Forever 21 is one of the biggest clothing brands on Earth, after all.

This is the psychology of pop culture America: we like to throw away the things we love before they wither. We buy records and films from brand new stars fresh out of their teens, and with our next dollar, we buy the tabloids that skewer them for their addictions, their divorces, their cellulite, their depression, or their suicide. Build them up, then tear them down.

But that is not all there is to it. Thinking about the 27 club is also about appreciating how totally unique and unfathomable each human experience is—how nature and nurture lead us on twin leashes toward futures we never imagined. Understanding another person's pain, what drives them to do things that we find inexplicable, is much like understanding another's perception of the color blue... How do we really know if my blue is the same as your blue? What if what you call blue would be totally unrecognizable to me? How can we come to an understanding if I'll never *really* know what your blue looks like? This concept applies to everything: Can we ever possibly know, can we ever get close enough to truly understand, the motivations, the neurochemical reactions, the environment, and the history that lead to each personal decision we make in life? When you're in the midst of talking to someone, this is not usually how we think about them, because engaging with someone on any level in real time is an emotional act. When you see someone jumping into the deep end of the lake, you try to stop them, because it's too dangerous. Or, perhaps, you're the one jumping, and you get annoyed that the "square" behind you is trying to prevent you from living life to its fullest. But both of those people arrived at their opposing views of the same act through their own life experience, through the prism of who they are, and it may not be possible to truly exchange perspectives in that moment, or any.

True understanding may always elude us. Certainly, it has eluded me; there are people I will probably never understand, people with whom I have been very close, and people of whom I have been very critical. My bandmates are an example. My children are another—they would be the first to admit that we never quite understand one another. There is always a personal and generational gap.

However, that's what this book should be: an attempt to understand (for the first time, in my case) what makes people who are in the same position as me, here at "the top," go down a darker road. For the first time in my life, I'm going to (for the most part) withhold my criticisms, especially on the subject of substance abuse, and just try to get inside the heads of these figures, because we share so many things and yet ended up in such different places, in the end.

I grew up in this business, the business of "celebrity," and I've seen young people fall victim to a strange pattern. It doesn't get everyone. Maybe it doesn't even get most. But there is something, it seems, that makes people at the top of a mountain want to go to the edge and peer into the void. Sometimes, they fall accidentally. Sometimes the mob pushes them. And, sometimes, they jump. Like all clichés, "It's lonely at the top" sprouts from an authentic human experience, which perhaps only a small section of the populace will ever get to encounter. There are people, for myriad reasons, who can reach the pinnacle of success, be surrounded by friends and fans who adore them, but who nevertheless feel *alone* in ways other people do not. There is a paradoxical isolation in being surrounded, for some people. It's something I have never experienced. But many people in my same position have.

To me, that is what the 27 club really is: a pattern that emerges from the strange impulse that too many young people, so full of potential, cannot help but feel, just by the nature of who they are and what they have experienced. I was never immune, *per se*, to this morbid fascination, but I was only ever a spectator to it. I always wanted to know what caused people, some of whom I knew, peripherally, to fall so far, so fast. I wanted to know why certain people felt that way, while some of our other contemporaries seemed perfectly comfortable with the attention, able to grow a thick skin and ignore the frothing critics. Some survived by luck, despite their self-destructive behavior, and some, like me, never partook in the more dangerous parts of the lifestyle.

A related, but separate, issue to the misplaced romance of self-destruction is false equivalency when it comes to different definitions of "rebellion." When I was young, to rebel was to champion outlandish ways of dressing, casual sex, and other nontraditional lifestyle choices. In other words: to rebel was to be free of those traditions that did not make sense to you, no matter who of the older generation expected you to follow them. Freedom was the reason for it all; the freedom to pursue the life one wants. However, in my opinion, rebellion has become grafted onto self-destruction, and soon freedom is not enough; soon one has to balance oneself on the edge of losing everything, including freedom, in order to be free. The unfortunate old adage, "sex, drugs, and rock 'n' roll," has been romanticized to such a degree that we all accept it without thinking twice. I believe that the "drugs" part of this mantra has, quite literally, contributed to hundreds, maybe thousands, of young deaths across the world. And it continues to do so—in different forms, and in different genres of music.

Now, I've been outspoken about never drinking or doing any drugs, period. To me, it was not a difficult decision to make; the information about the risks was there and seemed to me to be plainly logical. But for many, this decision was clearly not as easy as it was for me. Some, perhaps, did not think much at all, and merely went with the cultural flow—the influencing or enabling forces that almost all young people feel. I've rarely minced words on the topic, and my harsh tongue has got me into trouble on occasion, when I have chosen to speak out.

Certainly, it is worth noting that for most of my adult life I did not know a *thing* about major depressive disorder or its related conditions. I didn't believe it was real, nor could I understand what it was actually like. It just seemed like a "rich person problem" to me, a consequence of the cushy life my generation built for my children's generation. I've learned more about it since, and have changed my mind, though sometimes it is admittedly still hard for me to grasp. I've met people and become close with people who deal with mental health problems. I can be a bonehead sometimes, but I've always prided myself on being someone who is open to changing my mind at the introduction of new evidence.

Many people familiar with me may be surprised by my change of heart. The catalyst for this project was a series of very long, involved conversations with my son Nick, who is helping me write and edit the book. Nick and I disagree on a great many things. We talk, hash things out, and sometimes never find any common ground. Our life experiences are different, but so are our minds in a lot of crucial ways. But we learn from each other; the first version of this book was going to be much more of a judgment piece, a criticism, until Nick began to talk to me about his experience interacting with some of the people involved. Nick had played with Robby Krieger of the Doors, and has had conversations with others peripheral to these stories. After we talked, I decided that the goal of this book should not be to chastise people or project my own views, but to simply understand—to dive deep into the lives of these icons whose work I loved, from the perspective of a fellow musician, a fellow public figure, and a fan.

The first time I realized I had something to learn was during one of these conversations with Nick. My son was troubled, which puzzled me; he had everything, in my view, that anyone could ever want. He lives a privileged, fortunate life, which I was able to give him a head start on. He works hard, and he's very aware of his luck. He goes out of his way to express gratitude for even the smallest conveniences his life offers, and he tries to earn them too. And yet, I found that he was very distraught. When he called me, very shaken up, I tried to remind him about all the things he had going for him, as I often do: he had a great family, he had his health, he had a wonderful life—there was no reason for him to be sad. He said that he knew all of that, and he was grateful. So I asked him why, and he said there was no reason; he was just having an episode. "It's in my head, like a stomach ache is in your stomach," he said. "I'm not dissatisfied with life. My brain just does this sometimes."

Sometimes it takes someone that you love to explain things to you before you can believe they are real. That was my first encounter with this strange thing, clinical depression, that I actually considered to be authentic. And he needed me to feel that way. He told me: "All I need from you, the only way you can help me, is for you to believe me...believe that I'm not just making this up."

I told him, "I do. I believe you. I've seen it," and I had. Though I had brushed people off in the media, regarding those I did not know personally, I could not brush off a family member. It has made me reflect on other cases I've perhaps been too quick to dismiss. I didn't understand what this thing called "depression" was. I thought it was just an emotion, like any other emotion, and thus a part of someone's character. In a way, I will never fully understand. But that is the point—I do not need to understand. I only need to understand that they arrived in that place the same way anyone arrives anywhere, at the behest of a whirlwind of forces beyond our control, many of which have to do with genes. I also need to learn to trust people when they try to communicate their pain.

Once I realized my son was part of this thing, it made me regret things I had said publicly about depression and its related issues. I have been harsh because I didn't *believe* that people could be sick in *that* way. I believed it was a matter of willpower, a matter of character flaws, and I suspect many in my generation still feel this way. Again, a kernel of truth: of course there *are* people who simply need to toughen up and start taking their lives seriously. But mixed in with these unmotivated, healthy individuals are people who really are tormented by a medical, psychological condition outside of their control. I never would have changed my point of view on this had it not affected someone close to me. And that is my flaw.

I want this to be an olive branch to people whose choices I don't necessarily approve of. The meaning of that olive branch is that we can try to understand each other without condoning actions we don't believe in. There is a way we can guide the people (especially children and young people) who look up to us and help them realize how they, in each of their unique ways, can live better and longer than we do.

So I offer no apologies for my disapproval of drugs, only context, and some explanation regarding what I mean when I criticize people who abuse drugs. That is the following:

My point of view, as of today, is that if you are a well-informed, healthy adult, and you choose to take that first hit of heroin, that *first* hit is your responsibility. If you know the risks and dangers of an activity and choose to partake in it anyway, my sympathies are difficult to muster. I used to say that without reservation and without caveat.

But, I also know that to err is human—a lesson I learned from very personal, as well as public experience. So perhaps there is more room for more nuance here than I've admitted on-the-air.

My critique, obviously, does not apply to children—who don't know any better, and who are perhaps exposed to a dealer, an enabler, or an otherwise bad influence that gets them into something dangerous from a young age. It also does not apply to people with undiagnosed mental health problems, who self-medicate for lack of hope or other options. As I've said, I've often painted depression with too broad a brush out of anger and frustration. I came from the "Pull yourself up by your bootstraps" generation; there simply was no conversation about depression, nor public understanding of what it means, at least not in the circles in which I ran. Depression was treated as a personality flaw. "Get over it" is a phrase I heard a lot from adults growing up, and it's a lesson I internalized and regurgitated to people in turn.

It worked for me. It made me toughen up and make my dreams come true. I still find myself skeptical of people's motivations when they claim they are unable to function because of their emotions, because, although I now acknowledge depression exists, liars and scam artists exist as well, and liars and scam artists will take advantage of a real condition, like depression, in order to excuse themselves from the responsibilities of life. Depressive people are real, and slackers are real, and sometimes it's hard to tell the difference.

The difference between addiction and any other personal problem—the fact that exposure to drugs is, more often than not, a decision an individual makes—is why the concept that addiction is a sickness is difficult for people to comprehend. This moment of choice, and this informed, healthy, pre-drug person is what I have

been referring to when I've been dismissive and angry
with people who struggle with addiction in the past.
And my point of view has evolved since then to include
extenuating circumstances I hadn't thought about before.

But I stand by this specific flag I've planted.
From heroin to cigarettes, coffee, gambling, junk food,
and social media, we all know (especially in this age of
information we live in) what these things can do to a
person when they get out of control. There is an element
of personal responsibility there. It has always frustrated
me that people who *get* sober get applause, while people
who never touched the stuff in the first place get apathy.

But context is key. Before people become
rock stars, there are checks and balances in their
lives—maybe parents or concerned friends, talking in
their ear and intervening. Or, perhaps it's the fear of
consequences, of getting arrested, that keep "ordinary"
people from going off the deep end. For young people,
these limitations are annoyances, even though they save
them from themselves.

Once you climb to the top of the mountain,
however, the unfortunate by-product is that there are
very few checks and balances. This I say from personal
experience. When you reach a certain level of fame, the
people around you will only tell you what you want to
hear. I hope the dangers of living in an echo chamber,
in this age of political unrest and failed conversations,
is obvious. Fame takes that echo chamber and further
insulates it from all outside influence. And when you
have enough power and money to do whatever you like,

whenever you like, the only true consequences, the only true laws, are natural laws.

Let's just say it plainly, as if for the first time: drug and alcohol abuse kills people. It hurts people, and it breaks up families, friends…and bands. However, everyone—*everyone*—has demons, whether they are aware of them or not. If there is anything I've learned as I get older, it is that I am not as rock-solid as I once thought I was when it comes to being hijacked by my demons.

My problem was never drugs, but I have my own "drugs" that I am loath to admit as problems and that haunt me in different ways. Attention, accolades, success, validation, even chocolate cake—these are the "drugs" to which I am addicted. Admitting this has made it easier for me to empathize with those whose internal issues are different than mine. I may never understand their nature, but I can understand that they exist, and believe that they are real.

The main reason I never acknowledged my demons before is probably the same reason that famous figures who have substance abuse problems have a hard time grappling with their issues: the problem of the yes-men. After all, who will tell the rock star, the icon, the rebel, the hero, at the peak of his power and influence, *what to do*? Who's going to tell a cultural monarch, a creative revolutionary, to put the glass, the pipe, the needle down, to change something about themselves, when there are hordes of young people outside telling them to keep going exactly as they are?

My life and career in the rock 'n' roll industry has

been plagued by inconvenience at best, and tragedy at worst, because of other people's decisions regarding the abuse of drugs. Addicts have hung in grim orbit around me my entire professional life. I've lost friends, partners, and opportunities because of drug abuse, and that, if I'm being candid, is probably where my frustration and intolerance comes from. In the end, when I react in anger to drugs, it's because of what I've seen them do to people I care about. It's a defense mechanism. When I have seen a friend or an associate making that choice, I want to grab them by the scruff of their neck and slap some sense into them. I still, perhaps, will never understand that decision—that first decision, not the ones that are the result of being helpless to addiction, which come afterwards. We cannot control addiction; many are powerless to it. *Getting* addicted, for the first time, however—perhaps we can control that. And when I see a friend going down that road, my emotions overcome me. I want to save them from themselves. I get angry. Furious. I still feel this way, when I see it. So, once again; no apologies, only clarification.

Bearing all of this in mind, this book will attempt to discuss various cultural figures, within and beyond the music industry, who passed away at 27 years old, and try to make sense of and empathize with them. I will speculate about what forces, internal and external, led these young people down the wrong path, as well as what their lives and their deaths meant to the culture surrounding them. Most of this book will not be an argument for or against anything; it will simply be an attempt to understand. Much of it will be biography, simple observation, and reflection from my vantage point. But I am hoping my point of view will, in some small way, count as firsthand, from within the eye of the storm, and will add a new perspective to this old discussion. In a way, I want to break the spell and show that, even without self-destruction, the people listed in this book were great at what they did. Young death, mental turmoil, and struggles with addiction should add no extra sheen to their legacies, and should not be the entire focus of their stories. On the contrary, our mourning should be properly mournful, not asterisked with that strange caveat: how *cool* it is to hit a wall. Perhaps if we internalize that the charisma of death is a myth, the next generation of young icons won't feel the need to continue the trend, and can start their own revolutions and actually see them through to the end. Perhaps if we focus more on life than death, we can actually understand these figures as people. If we glamorize anything, let it be the work and the humanity of these artists, not the dirty laundry and juicy gossip.

It seems to me that young people with dreams of greatness are given a burden: a viral narrative that to self-destruct (in one way or another) in order to achieve a sort of mythical greatness is the right way to go; that this is the only thing that makes one valuable and desirable and heroic. We mythologize famous deaths as, "Burning too bright, for half as long." Many people believe their status as "great" is causally related to this self-destruction. I don't believe this. To me, our fascination with this pattern, the age 27, is the result of our need to ascribe some meaningful narrative to the absurdity of life, to take the sting out of death. In reality, these artists were people, as messy and flawed and absurd as all people are—as I am, as you are. And every person's experience is unique, incomparable, and worth exploring.

So, as if for the first time, let us be fascinated more than we are judgmental. Let us try to understand them not as heroes or villains, gods or icons, good or bad influences, but simply, as human beings.

Robert Johnson

1911 – 1938

"Me and the Devil, walkin' side by side."

—ROBERT JOHNSON[8]

8   "Me and the Devil Blues," by Robert Johnson (US: 1937), Vocalion Records, prod. Don Law.

Robert Johnson

Any respectable list of the greatest pop and rock artists will begin with a blues artist, and any list of the best blues artists puts Robert Johnson somewhere near the top.

The scope of Johnson's influence on music and culture is difficult to quantify, and perhaps seems surprising at first listen. His recordings are raw, live, grainy, and simple, as most blues was at the time. But an intangible charisma and rawness—as well as unceasing urban myths about Faustian bargains with the devil—have cemented Johnson as a feature of Americana for decades. Among those who list Johnson as a direct influence, if not personal hero, are: Eric Clapton, Keith Richards, Jimmy Page, Bob Dylan, Fleetwood Mac, The Allman Brothers Band, and countless more household names. All this longevity from a musician with only two verified photographs, a notoriously elusive biography, little success in his time, and just a handful of recordings to his name.

Johnson's personal history is shrouded in – mystery, and only the skeleton of his life story can actually be unearthed, the details lost to hearsay and shoddy record-keeping. He was known to have married twice, although the dates are disagreed upon. He haunted juke joints—informal music establishments that were frequented by African Americans in the South— and was the protégé of legendary bluesman Son House (1902–1988), from whom the most valuable firsthand accounts of Johnson come. The rest, it seems, is difficult to pin down; so many dates involved in his personal timeline are surrounded by the chatter of rumor, legend, and contradiction.

The world was a more dangerous place for a black man in America between 1911 and 1938, when Johnson lived, and this background of terror can be heard in many of his lyrics, and in his tormented wailing. What we do know is that he was born in Mississippi, and had many (half) siblings. He was an illegitimate child; his mother Julia was married to Charles Dodds, a sharecropper, but his real father was a plantation worker named Noah Johnson. Young Robert was sent to live with Dodds in Memphis when his siblings were grown, after Dodds had fled his plot of land in Mississippi when threatened by a lynch mob.[9] Johnson began to learn guitar in Memphis, before he was sent back to his mother (and her new husband). Johnson apparently wanted to play the blues from before the age of nine, rejecting the safer, rural life his stepfather championed.

He married in his late teens, to an even younger girl named Virginia Travis, who died in childbirth not long afterwards. Relatives of the girl in the 1992 documentary *The Search for Robert Johnson* reported that they believed her death to be "divine punishment" for Johnson's ambition to sing nonreligious songs, a crime that they termed, "selling his soul to the devil."[10] Johnson, according to researcher Robert "Mack" McCormick, speaking in the documentary, did not necessarily mind the description of his goal; he was, after all, thoroughly resolved to play worldly songs as opposed to following the spiritual, domestic farm life the rest of his community expected of him.

One can see how the more infernal legends surrounding Johnson began to take shape, even at that early stage. Little did they know, it seemed, how tantalizing these satanic rumors about Johnson's life would be to his musical inheritors. His "damnation" would only serve to bolster his legend. Still, it must have been exceedingly traumatic to be blamed,

---

9   *Searching for Robert Johnson: The Life and Legend of "The King of Delta Blues Singers,"* by Peter Guralnick (Plume, US: 1998)
10   *The Search for Robert Johnson* (UK, 1992), dir. Chris Hunt, prod. Iambic Productions/Film4, 72 min.

supernaturally, for your wife's death in childbirth.

Johnson sought out mentors, and his learning curve was apparently quite steep. Perhaps the most pivotal turning point in Johnson's life was the arrival of legendary bluesman Son House to the Mississippi Delta—the flat, fertile floodplain that was covered in cotton plantations and became the birthplace of American blues. A 19-year-old Johnson (who apparently had a baby face, as House mistook him for 16) would follow his hero to every Robinsonville juke joint he could, sitting cross-legged on the floor between House and guitar player Willie Brown (1900–1952), soaking in every note like a sponge.[11] House recalled:

> When we'd leave at night to go play for the balls, he'd slip off and go over to where we were. His mother and stepfather didn't like for him to go out on those Saturday night balls because the guys were so rough. But he'd slip away anyway. Sometimes he'd even wait until his mother went to bed and then he'd get out the window and make it to where we were. He'd get where Willie [Brown] and I were and sit right down on the floor and watch from one to the other.[12]

Initially, House was not impressed by his would-be student. Johnson would often bother House and

11   *Preachin' the Blues: The Life and Times of Son House,* by Daniel Beaumont (Oxford UP, UK: 2011)
12   Ibid.

Brown about getting stage time, and borrow their guitars when they went out for a smoke, without asking for anyone's permission:

> He blew a harmonica and he was pretty good with that, but he wanted to play guitar…and such a racket you never heard! It'd make people mad, you know. They'd come [outside] and say, "Why don't ya'll go in there and get that guitar away from that boy?" I'd scold him about it, "Don't do that, Robert. You drive the people nuts. You can't play nothing." Still, he didn't care how I'd get after him about it. He'd do it anyway.[13]

Johnson was not discouraged by his hero's bad review. He begged House for lessons, and he eventually agreed to help him. He then traveled for a year, playing as many juke joints (and even street corners) as he could. Eventually, he returned, and House heard him play once more.

This time, it was different. "He was so good. When he finished, all our mouths were standing open," House recalled.[14]

His stage presence had reportedly improved as well. "The story goes that he would often concentrate his performance on one woman in the audience; a risky business in a world where men were happy to fight

13   Ibid.
14   Ibid.

when they felt aggrieved," [15] wrote Richard Havers. This, apparently, was only one of his trademarks; the other, which seems to contradict the first, was that he would sit facing the corner of the wall. Some said this was due to extreme shyness, while others insisted that the angle of the walls would work as a natural, acoustic amplifier.

This mysterious interim, between Johnson leaving the Delta and returning with a new, extraordinary talent, is where Johnson's story veers from the factual into the mythical. The basic premise of the myth goes, more or less, like this: Johnson, with his determination to achieve the greatness of House and others, was told (it is unclear by whom) to take his guitar to a certain crossroads at midnight. Where this crossroads exists, if it does, is a matter of disagreement; there is a tourist attraction in Clarksdale, Mississippi, which I have visited, that claims to be the genuine article, but many other accounts dispute this. At this crossroads, he meets a mysterious man, who tunes Johnson's guitar, plays it for a moment, then hands it back to Johnson. This magically imbues Johnson with inhuman musical ability, charisma, and fame, in exchange for his immortal soul. [16]

The legend of a bluesman selling his soul to the devil in exchange for musical greatness was, by that time, already well-known, and Johnson's rapid improvement in skill during this short time fit too conveniently into

---

15   "The Devil's Myth - The Myth of Robert Johnson," by Richard Havers, Udiscovermusic.com, 11/23/2016.
16   "Robert Johnson," Wikipedia.com, accessed: 04/11/2018.

the narrative—at least for those that wanted it to believe it. According to folklorists Barry Lee Pearson and Bill McCulloch: "Everybody was so anxious to make this devil story true that they've been working on finding little details that can corroborate it." [17] The mysterious events surrounding Johnson's death would ensure that this anxiety would become a fever.

By 1936, Johnson got a chance to record his songs in Texas.[18] He succeeded in making "Terraplane Blues" a modest success—enough to earn a second recording session, which would turn out to be his last. He recorded a total of only 29 songs.

Two years later, on August 16th, Johnson died. That is what is known.

Now, for the contradicting details...

Needless to say, the death records of black people in the early 20th century were often incomplete or careless, and Johnson's is no different. His official death certificate claims incorrectly that he died of syphilis at age 26 (an age apparently *guessed* at by the County Registrar). Additionally, this note was handwritten on the back of the certificate, phrased like some macabre short story:

17   *Robert Johnson: Lost and Found*, by Barry Lee Pearson and Bill McCulloch (University of Illinois Press, US: 2008)
18   "Robert Johnson at 100, Still Dispelling Myths," by Joel Rose, NPR. org, 05/06/2011.

I talked with the white man on whose place this negro died and I also talked with a negro woman on the place. The plantation owner said the negro man, seemingly about 26 years old, came from Tunica two or three weeks before he died to play banjo at a negro dance given there on the plantation. He stayed in the house with some of the negroes saying he wanted to pick cotton. The white man did not have a doctor for this negro as he had not worked for him. He was buried in a homemade coffin furnished by the county. The plantation owner said it was his opinion that the man died of syphilis. [19]

For anyone familiar with Johnson's life, the errors are plain to see. Most notably, his age, his playing a "banjo" as opposed to a guitar (which is not impossible, but does seem to raise a red flag), and most importantly, the fact that his cause of death was determined to be syphilis because "the plantation owner said it was his *opinion*" that it was so.

Alternatively, according to fellow musicians David "Honeyboy" Edwards (1915–2011) and Sonny Boy Williamson (1914–1938), influential bluesmen in their own right, who were reportedly present for Johnson's death, Johnson was actually murdered by a jealous juke joint owner who found out that Johnson had been

---

19   *Robert Johnson, Mythmaking, and Contemporary American Culture*, by Patricia R. Schroeder (University of Illinois Press, US: 2004)

sleeping with his wife.[20] Williamson claims that the man poisoned a bottle of Johnson's whiskey—with strychnine, possibly, although this has also been debated. Mack McCormick concurs with this version of events, and at one point even claimed that he knew the name of the perpetrator, though he never released it.[21] According to Edwards, Robert Johnson had been performing and accepting free drinks from the audience all evening and was, by the end of the night, too ill to continue, though this was initially ascribed to simple overdrinking. Several days passed as Johnson kept to his room, vomiting blood and (according to Edwards), "crawling around like a dog and howling."[22] He is said to have died in severe pain. The location of his burial site, much like the tales of his life and death, is a matter of debate; there are several gravestones in different places that people claim to be the genuine article.

The devil and the crossroads myth, like most urban myths and folk tales, has no single origin. Johnson himself never actually sang about the encounter; his most famous song, "Cross Road Blues" (later famously covered by Eric Clapton and Cream) tells a harrowing tale of trying to "flag a ride," hitchhiking alone as the sun sets—a dangerous, but not uncommon situation for a black man to find himself in at the time—but the lyrics

---

20   Ibid.
21   *The Americana Revolution: From Country and Blues Roots to the Avett Brothers, Mumford & Sons, and Beyond*, by Michael Scott Cain (Rowman & Littlefield, US: 2017)
22   *Robert Johnson, Mythmaking*, by P. Schroeder (2004)

do not explicitly mention a Faustian deal, nor do the lyrics of "Hellhound on my Trail," or any others.

The first glimmer of the myth, in the form it exists in today, seems to have come from Son House himself. An article in 1966 by Pete Welding stated that Son House, "suggested in all seriousness that Johnson, in his months away from home, had 'sold his soul to the devil in exchange for learning to play like that.' " [23] Though Welding uses the expression "in all seriousness," it is still unclear whether this was a simple figure of speech or a declaration of something House literally believed. This is the only significant reference to the devil in the article, but it was small tidbits like these that proved enough to fuel the fire for decades to come, all the way to the present day.

The relationship between blues music and sinfulness was considered a given in Johnson's time. Everything that was not gospel was suspect, so a career in juke joints and blues naturally became associated with "adultery, fornication, gambling, lying, and drinking." [24] Reverend Booker Miller, a bluesman and friend of legendary bluesman Charley Patton (d.1938), phrased it best: "Them old folks did believe the devil would get you for playin' the blues and livin' like that." [25] Writer Alan Lomax remarked that "every blues fiddler, banjo picker, harp blower, piano strummer and guitar framer was, in

---

23 "Robert Johnson: Hell Hound on His Trail," by Pete Welding, DownBeat magazine, 1966.
24 *Chasin' That Devil Music: Searching for the Blues*, by Gayle Dean Wardlow (Backbeat Books, US: 1998)
25 Ibid.

the opinion of both himself and his peers, a child of the Devil, a consequence of the black view of the European dance embrace as sinful in the extreme." [26]

This, in my opinion, is the embryonic stage of the worldview that later became the "sex, drugs, and rock 'n' roll" culture that we are now so familiar with. The true beginning of the 27 club phenomenon lies here: the idea that the pursuit of music, or fame and greatness generally, must include tantalizing danger, and that great worldly pleasure must always be linked to some sort of "evil," some sort of Monkey's Paw-type consequence. These ideas, to my personal bewilderment, seem to have stood the test of time, but I think they are unnecessary. Johnson did not have a choice to live in a dangerous world. He was born with black skin in America, in the early 20th century, and that was that. Things were dangerous enough for him already, without divine intervention. The fact that we fetishize this danger (from the comfort of our armchairs) proves we are missing the point at the heart of the blues, which is: a *protest* of unfair circumstances.

In terms of marketing, Johnson himself appeared, surprisingly, to be on my side of the fence: he knew that association with infernal imagery would "heighten his reputation among record buyers and juke house frolickers." [27] This formula works, and I as well as others in the music world have been inspired by this strategy

26   *The Land Where Blues Began*, by Alan Lomax (The New Press, US: 2002)

27   *Chasin' That Devil Music*, Wardlow (1998)

ever since. My "demon" persona, Alice Cooper and
Marilyn Manson's face paint, lyrics, and onstage antics,
Black Sabbath and Judas Priest's imagery, Led Zeppelin's
preoccupation with pagan symbology and Aleister
Crowley, the Rolling Stones giving "sympathy for the
devil," were all attempts at courting the same kind of
mythic, dangerous intrigue. Most of us do not actually
believe in the supernatural; this should go without saying.
But, nonetheless, the imagery is captivating, mysterious,
dangerous—and it scares people's parents, which, of
course, delighted the teenagers who bought our records.
This formula, like almost everything in modern music,
we owe to bluesmen like Robert Johnson. They are the
beginning of it all.

Did Johnson only become a legend *because* he
died young, under mysterious circumstances? I think
his story proves that this is not the case. The legends of
his skill had already begun to circulate, long before he
passed away. Rumors of demonic interference aside, he
stood out in terms of skill alone: "To the uninitiated,
Johnson's recordings may sound like just another dusty
Delta blues musician wailing away. But a careful listen
reveals that Johnson was a revisionist in his time [...]
Johnson's tortured soul vocals and anxiety-ridden guitar
playing aren't found in the cotton-field blues of his
contemporaries." [28] It is a shame, then, that we will never
get to see what else he may have produced, what further
universes of influence he would have created, had he

---

28   "Still Standing at the Crossroads," by Marc Myers, *Wall Street Journal*,
05/22/2011.

been given the opportunity to grow old. For Johnson, especially, among all the figures discussed in this book, we cannot blame him for his death. We can only blame his dangerous environment, and be glad he left behind what he did in spite of everything. Johnson's death as a young man was far and away the least interesting thing about his history, and his legend.

Brian
Jones

1942 – 1969

"Let's face it. The future as a Rolling Stone is very uncertain."

—BRIAN JONES[29]

29   "The 'Rolling Stones' Off the Record: Outrageous Opinions and Unrehearsed Interviews," by Mark Paytress (Omnibus Press, UK: 2005)

Brian
Jones

The story of Brian Jones, like many on this list, is the story of Icarus: a man who flew to excessive heights, heights that he was not prepared to handle, and paid the price for it. Jones was reportedly a man split down the middle: one half creativity, ambition, and the kind of proactive drive that makes things happen in business, and in life; the other half one of self-sabotage, inner conflict, poor decision-making, addiction, and bombastic behavior.

He founded, named, and was by many estimations the driving force behind one of the greatest rock 'n' roll bands in history: the Rolling Stones. He lived large and, as a result, pushed his body's tolerance to its breaking point. If this gives us any idea just how far he pushed, consider that Keith Richards (b.1943) and Mick Jagger (b.1943), notorious for their drug-fueled excesses, found him too much to handle. And yet, in the beginning, Jones was the rising tide that lifted all of their boats.

He was a multi-instrumentalist, playing a wide variety of nontraditional instruments from an early age. He was lucky enough to be born to musical parents in the small English town of Cheltenham in Gloucestershire County in 1944. His mother was a piano teacher and his father played guitar, keys, and harmonica. Like Amy Winehouse, Jones was rebellious and a true individual, and like Jim Morrison, he was book smart, and able to receive good grades with minimal effort or interest. He was expelled from Cheltenham Grammar School for "starting a rebellion against the prefects." [30] He also fathered several children in his late-teens and early-20s, before the Stones were even a hypothetical.

He tried to immerse himself in music, and worked odd jobs, such as being a coal-lorry (truck) driver to make ends meet. At around the same time, Jones was searching high and low for collaborators with whom he could make his musical dreams a reality. Jones was the original founder, the first one who put ads in the paper seeking out players in an attempt to start the band, a process that (after a few unsuccessful attempts) eventually attracted the attention of childhood friends Jagger and Richards. Jones was on the phone with venue owners before the band even had a name, pushing to secure a gig. He was the one that came up with the name "the Rolling Stones" on a whim, while on one of these phone calls, after seeing

30   "Brian Jones: Sympathy for the Devil," Rolling Stone editors, *Rolling Stone*. 09/09/1969.

the back of a Muddy Waters (1913–1983) record out of the corner of his eye, which read, "Rollin' Stone Blues." [31] Split second, impulsive decisions seemed to work out for him, or so it seemed in the beginning.

Jones pushed the band, fervently, to play gigs, to be seen, to put themselves out there. In the early days, he was the most eager stone to get rolling, doing double duty as bandmate and manager. Like many groups of that time period, the Rolling Stones began their career playing blues and R&B covers, inspired by the likes of Chuck Berry (1926–2017), Howlin' Wolf (1910–1976), Little Richard (b.1932), and of course, Robert Johnson.

As the Stones ascended, Jagger and Richards became closer to each other, and Jones began to drift away from them. In retrospect, it is hard to imagine anyone but Jagger or Richards being the largest head on the Stones' Rushmore, but Brian Jones was, for a short time, just as much of a focal point of the group. In the beginning, he was a heartthrob as much as Jagger. If you don't believe me, go check out the relative sizes of their heads and distance from the camera on the cover of the early album *Out of Our Heads*, as well as *Big Hits (High Tide and Green Grass)*, *Aftermath*, and *December's Children*. It goes without saying that Jagger was almost never in the background again—the later album, *Goat's Head Soup*, featured a closeup of *only* his face. But, in the early days, Jones was neck-and-neck for the coveted title of "the pretty one."

31   "Celebrity Deaths That Changed Music History: Gone Too Soon," by David Browne, RollingStone.com, 08/14/2017.

Jones' already extravagant drug use continued to interfere with aspects of the band's business—a story almost all musicians are familiar with, either from being that person or *dealing* with that person. I am no exception. It affects everything: productivity, creativity, social interactions with your bandmates. Everything. For those it hits hard, it has the opposite effect that all these myths of genius would have you believe: It destroys your creativity. It reverts you to second infancy. Author Gary Herman remarked that Jones was "literally incapable of making music; when he tried to play harmonica his mouth started bleeding." [32]

Said Jagger:

> Keith and I took drugs, but Brian took too many drugs of the wrong kind and he wasn't functioning as a musician. You certainly didn't know if he was gonna turn up and in what state he was gonna be in and then what he was gonna be able to do in that state... And then one time, when we sat around on the floor, we played in a circle, playing "No Expectations," and he picked up the guitar and played a very pretty lines [sic] on it, which you can hear on the record, and that was the last thing I remember him doing that was Brian.[33]

32   *Rock 'n' Roll Babylon: 50 Years of Sex, Drugs, and Rock 'n' Roll*, by Gary Herman (Putnam/Plexus, US: 1982/2017)
33   *Crossfire Hurricane* (UK: 2012), dir. Brett Morgen. prod. Milkwood Films, 112 min.

He would have no-shows, mood swings, one moment pleasant and charismatic, the next entirely hostile, melancholy, or defeatist.[34] There was unrest brewing in the young man's heart that he had a hard time articulating to his friends and bandmates, and so the drugs became his confidant instead.

"My ultimate aim in life was never to be a pop star," Jones said. "I enjoy it with reservations. But I'm not really satisfied either artistically or personally," [35] he said during an interview.

His musical output dwindled. "He was already in 'bye-bye' land," [36] Richards said. On top of that, one of Jones' girlfriends left him for Richards, further destroying their ability to collaborate. Jones plunged even further into substance abuse to cope. His now multiple arrests for drug possession prevented him from acquiring visas to tour, and his contributions to the new album were minimal at best.

This, it seemed, was the last straw, and the rest of the band unanimously decided to part ways with him. The band that Jones had, by all accounts, created (and named) was finished with him, and he with it. Jagger reflects: "It was a very, very difficult decision to make. This was someone that you'd spent the beginning of the band with. He was the author of his own misfortunes, really, but when you look back on it now, you think surely

---

34   *Stone Alone: The Story of a Rock 'n' Roll Band*, by Bill Wyman (Da Capo Press, US: 1997)
35   *Crossfire Hurricane* (Morgen, 2012)
36   Ibid.

we could have done something. You know, did something more." [37] This story is tried and true, and has rippled in other bands before and after the Stones, including my own. It is always an impossible choice to make and yet, if you are in that position with a friend or a colleague that is deep into the dark hole that drugs dig for you, it is also equally impossible to keep things as they are. Immovable object, meet unstoppable force.

Not long after, Jones' then-girlfriend, Anna Wohlin, found him floating face down in his swimming pool, with the usual amounts of drug and drink in his blood. The Stones were told while they were in the studio with producer Jimmy Miller (1942–1994), and when someone broke the news to them, the collective response was ambivalence: "Everybody just looks at each other and goes, 'Finally.' It was almost like it was bound to happen, one way or another," [38] said Richards.

Echoes of one of his blues heroes, Robert Johnson, abound after his death. There are those who claim he was murdered, and conspiracy theories continue to spread, which Wohlin concurs with: "Brian is still portrayed as a bitter, worn-out and depressed man who was fired because of his drug habit, and who died because he was drunk or high," she said. "But my Brian was a wonderful, charismatic man who was happier than ever, had given up drugs and was looking forward to pursuing the musical career he wanted. I knew all along

---

37   *Crossfire Hurricane* (Morgen, 2012)
38   Ibid.

he did not die a natural death. I'm still sure of it." [39]

Young people all over the world, especially in London, mourned. This I find to be darkly ironic, as these same young people probably cheered the outlandishness of his drug-fueled antics just weeks before.

As the Stones' official history has progressed, Jones' legacy has been steadily minimized—whether fairly or unfairly depending on who you ask. Biographer Paul Trynka, author of *Brian Jones: The Making of the Rolling Stones*, believes that, "History is written by the victors," and that in retelling the band's legacy, the other members often forget to mention that Jones was the true genesis of it all.[40]

As we go on, notice the difference in the way Wohlin describes his death and reputation above, versus how the press described it in the following quote from Jones' obituary in *Rolling Stone* magazine in 1969: "What the Stones as a group sang about, what Jagger and Richard [sic] wrote about, Jones did, and he did it right out in public, and he got caught, and he looked the part. Paternity suits even in the early days, dope busts, pink suits, chartreuse suits, the bell of yellow hair and the impish grin, even the red and yellow stripes he wore…" [41]

There are a few things to notice about this quote, but what sticks out most to me is the fact that "dope busts" and "paternity suits" are listed in the same breath, with

---

39   "The Day That Rolling Stones Co-Founder Brian Jones Was Found Dead," by Corbin Reiff, UltimateClassicRock.com, 2015.
40   *Brian Jones: The Making of the Rolling Stones*, by Paul Trynka (Plume, US: 2015)
41   "*Obituary: Brian Jones*," by Greil Marcus, *Rolling Stone*, 09/09/1969.

the same tone and gravity (or lack thereof), as the color of his suit, how nice his hair and smile were, his consistent integrity. This, to me, is the epitome of the 27 club mentality, and what makes the myth, at times, corrosive: that moment when self-destruction becomes a fashion statement as opposed to a problem, a sickness, something to worry about, particularly if you love someone, even from afar. His partners, Richards and Jagger, were also lauded by the cool crowd for being "dangerous." These two aspects of their legend go hand in hand to this day. It is only by luck, perhaps in genetics or simple random chance, in my opinion, that Jagger and Richards survived to their current old age and Jones didn't. Brian was less lucky—something in his body composition or his genetics or the dosage or the frequency made him more susceptible to the very same lifestyle choices his colleagues made. Still, no distinction was made; he was encouraged all the same. "Sure, he died," the fans seem to say, "but man, what a *rebel. How cool.*" Whether or not we admit it, that reckless voice exists in the back of every young person's head when they shoot for fame and fortune.

"You see, you're thrust into the limelight in a youth-orientated thing," said Jagger, in an interview on their 50th anniversary for the documentary *Crossfire Hurricane.* "It's not about growing up. It's about not growing up, in a way. Then it's about bad behavior. Then you're about bad behavior. So then you start behaving badly." [42] Richards, in the same interview: "It's a weird

42   *Crossfire Hurricane* (Morgen, 2012)

situation…if you do something wrong, even better." [43]

This behavior by someone with fewer dollars (or, in this case, pounds) to their name would be evidence that they need intervention, that they do not have a good hold on life. But, in a rock star? These things are looked at as icing on the cake. "Those drugs were a great interest to the press and the general public," [44] said Jagger. Richards remarked that getting thrown in jail on a drug bust for LSD "cemented our relationships with the public, and it sort of gave us a badge of honor in a way, you know. You've basically given me a license now. It was Jesse James time." [45]

This stuff snuck in, slyly, alongside the awesome power of music, sexual liberation, and social unrest, as though self-destruction and healthy rebellion against authority must go hand in hand. That conflation is the beginning of what leads these young people to implode at such a tender age. "Hurt yourself," the mob and the fans seem to say, "and we will love you all the more for it." It may have been who he was before the world knew his name; he made his own mistakes, of that we can be sure. But was it healthy, was it right, that the more the Stones soared, the more Jones was encouraged to plunge ever farther down by his culture, his fans, and rock journalism, those voices that grin slyly and goad someone teetering on the edge just so they can catch a glimpse of what they are not brave or foolish or rich enough

43   Ibid.
44   Ibid.
45   Ibid.

to attempt themselves? Remember: these guys were just kids—late-teens into early-20s. What chance did they have to resist the lure of the false belief that every beautiful woman in the world would want them and love them if they would only pick up a guitar in one hand and a syringe in the other? "In a way, I kind of felt that everyone else was writing a script for me," said Richards. "'You're going to do what I can't.' Okay. That's a very easy role to slip into. There's a slot available, and it was built just for me." [46] The *Rolling Stone* obituary went on: "A few years ago there were a lot of songs written and a lot of questions asked about such things as 'Who Killed Davey Moore' and 'Who Killed Norma Jean' and so on. The answer, of course, was 'everybody.' " [47] Perhaps this is true. Trynka attributes Jones's "downfall to a conjunction of factors, some related to those character flaws but others external to him." [48]

As a fan, I would have wanted to see what was next, and I would have wanted to see him live a longer, happier life. He may not have been as prolific as Richards and Jagger in original compositions, although this is debated by Trynka, who quotes Stones accountant Stan Blackbourne as recalling, "I used to say to Brian, 'What on Earth are you doing? You write some of these songs, and you give the name over as if Mick Jagger has done it. Do you understand you're giving 'em thousands of pounds!' All the time I used to tell

46   Ibid.
47   "Obituary," Marcus, *Rolling Stone*, 1969.
48   "Ignobly Fading Away From the Rolling Stones: 'Brian Jones: The Making of the Rolling Stones,' a Biography," by Larry Rohter, *New York Times*, 11/19/2014.

him, 'You're writing a blank check.' " [49] Regardless of
nitpicking which songs, and when, and how much, what
Jones did do showed a reservoir of potential that will
never be tapped, because we all waited for the next story
of self-destructive debauchery. He obliged, and gave it
to us, and we lost him to it, in the same way we could
have lost any of the other Stones. Remember, Jimmy
Page (b.1944) left the Yardbirds and went on to form
Led Zeppelin. Eric Clapton (b.1945) left Cream, and
is still going. What could Brian Jones have done given
the chance? He was reportedly in talks about forming a
supergroup with John Lennon. Why do we fool ourselves
into thinking that the hard-partying was the part about
the Stones that matters? "Brian Jones got many things
wrong in his life, but the most important thing, he got
right," [50] said Larry Rohter. In my estimation, that would
be the music—the work.

"If I could stick a knife in my heart, suicide
right on stage," sings Jagger, "Would it be enough
for your teenage lust?" A good rock 'n' roll lyric, but
probably a response to a pressure Jagger really felt; we
do, unconsciously or not, demand a lot of self-harm from
these young kids who entertain us.

"If Keith Richards and Mick Jagger were the mind
and body of the Rolling Stones, Brian Jones," wrote *Rolling
Stone* magazine in 1969, "was clearly the soul."

---

49   Ibid.
50   Ibid.

Jimi Hendrix

1942 – 1970

"I don't really live on compliments... it has a way of distracting me. A whole lotta musicians and artists, they hear all these compliments and say, 'Wow I must have been really great.' So, they get fat and satisfied, and then they get lost, and they forget about the actual talent that they have."

—JIMI HENDRIX

Jimi Hendrix

I remember hearing about Jimi Hendrix when I was about 14 years of age. I was just starting to take a keen interest in music at that time, but I was too young to go to clubs and actually see the artists. My "Beatlemania" was just blossoming, and remains to this day.

As time passed, I started reading English music journals like *Melody Maker* and *New Music Express*. I noticed they all began to rave about this amazing new guitarist who played guitar with his teeth—a stunt that might seem a bit old hat now, but at the time was pretty outlandish.

I was a fan of the Animals at the time, and I learned that the Animals' bass player, Chas Chandler (1938–1996), had become Hendrix's manager, bringing him to London to record his first album. This was just an up-and-comer, and yet I was stunned at the amount of what I like to call "British royalty" that came to witness and pay homage to this phenomenon. The list was dizzying, and I'm not talking about the Queen. There they all were: The Beatles and Clapton, in the *audience*, not on stage, with their mouths wide open in awe. Something was different about Hendrix.

Like others in the know, I wasn't just a fan; I studied his stagecraft, his onstage persona, and though not well-known, I just might have got a certain idea about sticking my tongue out when I saw Hendrix performing his stylized cunnilingus on his air guitar.

Johnny Alan Hendrix was a child of Seattle, though he would not live long enough to see the grunge scene that his fellow club member, Cobain, would later champion in his hometown. When he wasn't in Seattle, or when his mother and father were having their various marital spats (some of which got violent enough that young Hendrix would hide in a closet), he would spend time on a reservation in Vancouver with his part-Cherokee grandmother. His brother, Leon, was in and out of the foster care system, though they tried to remain close, and his three other siblings were all given up for foster care not long after their birth. His mother Lucille had him when she was young, and Hendrix was nine years old when his parents finally divorced.

Not long after, Hendrix's mother passed away at 33 (when Hendrix was 10) of a ruptured spleen, made all the worse by cirrhosis of the liver.[51]

Hendrix's father, like many on this list, was a strict and religious man, demanding silence and respect from his son from the moment he was old enough to talk, and the young Hendrix was a quiet and subdued person due to this overbearing figure. His father reportedly refused to allow young Jimi to go to his mother's funeral, forcing the child and his brother to take Seagram's 7 whiskey shots, telling them "that was how men dealt with grief."[52]

This quiet personality, forced upon him by hardship and poverty, would stand in stark contrast to the explosive, liberating noise he would later produce with his voice and his instrument.

Like Robert Johnson before him, Hendrix was captivated by the blues from an early age. His favorites were Muddy Waters, Howlin' Wolf, Chuck Berry, and Buddy Holly. Though many people would focus on his race, Hendrix, early on, was simply focused on the sounds of the guitar: "Color just doesn't make any difference. Look at Elvis. He could sing the blues, and he was white. I always say, 'Let the best man win, whether you're black, white, or purple.'"[53]

While in school, Hendrix used to imitate playing a guitar on a broom he kept with him—this miming occurring, incredibly, before the term "air guitar" was

51   *Dead Gods: The 27 Club*, by Christopher Salewicz (Quercus Publishing, UK: 2015)
52   *Becoming Jimi Hendrix: From Southern Crossroads to Psychedelic London, The Untold Story of a Musical Genius*, by Stephen Robbie and Brad Schreiber (Da Capo, US: 2010)
53   *Jimi Hendrix: Voodoo Child* (UK, 2010), dir. Bob Smeaton, prod. Experience Hendrix LLC, 91 min.

popularized.[54] Later he found a ukulele with one string remaining in a neighbor's garage, and he attempted to teach himself Elvis songs by sounding them out:

> He did not realize it, but Jimi was following in the path of other great blues guitarists, such as Elmore James and B. B. King, who as children played what was called the "one strand on the wall." A single wire that held a broom together would be removed, straightened with a rock or other hard object, and then nailed to a wall or a back porch. The neck of a bottle became the slide, which produced a limited range of notes while the wire was plucked.[55]

His father bought him his first guitar, an acoustic, from a family friend for five dollars. This would be the first instance of having to reverse the order of the strings on a right-handed guitar, as was his famous signature. In this first case, it was because left-handed guitars were simply too expensive and too hard to find—a friend had to practically humiliate his father to pressure him into spending the money to buy his son an instrument at all.[56] Jimi was glued to the guitar night and day, once even taking a beating from bullies who tried to separate him from it, preferring to take the injuries than release his

54   *Becoming Jimi Hendrix* S. Robbie/B. Schreiber, (2010)
55   Ibid.
56   Ibid.

beloved instrument.[57] He was self-taught, studying his heroes, like Muddy Waters, and trying to play the way they played.

Though he did not struggle academically, Hendrix dropped out of school early. He dreamed, in his early years, of being an actor or a painter, and would sketch and paint in his free time, and read science fiction magazines and books (he apparently loved *Flash Thompson*). He began to work for his father's gardening business after he dropped out of school, and they struggled financially.

When he became a legal adult, he enlisted to be a paratrooper in the 101st Airborne at Fort Campbell, Kentucky, stating that he wanted to "get it over with"[58] so he could get started on a music career that wouldn't later be interrupted by a draft. He was nowhere near an ideal soldier, and both he and his superiors seemed to know that he did not belong there. However, in his letters to his father, he expressed a significant amount of pride at wearing the "screaming eagle" patch, and spoke of making his father and the rest of his family proud, though he apparently was only waiting for his opportunity to get out.[59] His military career was short-lived as he (allegedly) injured his ankle on a skyhook during training, 13 months in, allowing for his honorable discharge.

Afterward, he decided to pursue guitar-playing in Nashville. He lived in poverty and squalor as he

---

57   Ibid.
58   *Jimi Hendrix: Voodoo Child* (Smeaton, 2010)
59   Ibid.

recovered from his training injuries, and found himself surrounded by race riots and restaurants that refused to serve him. He would sometimes steal food to get by, along with receiving help from various women in his life. "I used to be on the block starving. Girls used to help me. Girls were my best friends." [60]

In the meantime, he gigged wherever he could, in clubs, restaurants, and on street corners. He once spent nearly all the 400 dollars to his name in a Clarksville bar, showing his relentless generosity and foreshadowing his later drinking: "I went in this jazz joint and had a drink. I liked it and I stayed. People tell me I get foolish, good-natured sometimes. Anyway, I guess I felt real benevolent that day. I must have been handing out bills to anyone that asked me. I came out of that place with 16 dollars left." [61]

He eventually formed a band with two friends and joined a few small tours in the South. As a black musician in the South, showmanship was more than a marketable skill—it was a survival strategy. It was during these sometimes tense shows that Hendrix, literally and figuratively, cut his teeth. "The idea of playing guitar with my teeth came to me in a town in Tennessee. Down there you have to play with your teeth or else you get shot. Those people really were hard to please. There's a trail of broken teeth all over the stage." [62]

The first glimmer of a break was when the

---

60   Ibid.
61   *Becoming Jimi Hendrix*, S. Robbie/B. Schreiber (2010)
62   *Jimi Hendrix: Voodoo Child* (Smeaton, 2010)

young Hendrix got a job playing in the backup band for a touring soul lineup featuring iconic singers Sam Cooke (1931–1964) and Solomon Burke (1940–2010). He toured the Midwest, then went on to win first place in an amateur night at the Apollo (first prize being 25 dollars). It was here that the Isley Brothers hired Hendrix to back them as well. From there, Hendrix quit to play with the legendary Little Richard (b.1932).[63] The archival photos and videos of Hendrix playing as a little-noticed backing musician are a sight to behold for anyone familiar with the brash, bright colors and stand-alone frontman charisma he became best known for. But even in these humble days, the icons Hendrix looked up to seemed to be sniffing out his potential, slowly moving him west. Hendrix, meanwhile, found himself in a boring, repetitive job. He disliked the uniformity of dress, and the lack of innovation he was allowed when playing other people's songs. He wanted to be up front. Hendrix himself had no way of knowing what was to come.[64]

Gradually, he made progress in his solo musical aspirations, eventually becoming a respectable session guitar player, backing the likes of Wilson Pickett (1941–2006), B.B. King (1925–2005), and Ike and Tina Turner.[65] He would also continue playing gigs with another original band of his in New York during this time.

An early, pivotal moment was when he befriended Chandler, and he saw Hendrix gig in Greenwich Village.

63   Ibid.
64   Ibid.
65   "Jimi Hendrix," Biography.com, accessed: 05/30/2018.

Chandler took Hendrix to London in 1966, ground zero of the British invasion, and it was there that Hendrix began to blossom into the innovator of blues and rock 'n' roll that he was always meant to be. Chandler helped him put together yet another band, The Jimi Hendrix Experience. "Hey Joe" was the first time Hendrix had tried to sing on record, and Chandler was proactive in encouraging Hendrix to start singing seriously.

The Jimi Hendrix Experience's debut album, *Are You Experienced,* went double platinum. Much of the album was created during on-the-spot jam sessions. Hendrix's lyrics took on a dreamy quality, and he claimed his was inspired partly by science fiction books he had read as a child (the name "Purple Haze" coming from a "purple death ray" he had seen in a sci-fi zine). Hendrix wanted the lyrics to be mythological, ambiguous, and open to interpretation.

At the suggestion of Paul McCartney (b.1942) (who, like many, had heard the rumors that had begun circulating in the States long before Hendrix actually returned to his home shores), The Experience played the Monterey Pop Festival, where Hendrix would play on the same stage as the rising star Janis Joplin. Brian Jones himself got on the mic to introduce Hendrix to his first big American crowd, describing him as, "A very good friend, a fellow countryman of yours, the biggest performer, the most exciting sounds I've ever heard." [66]

Hendrix would go on, infamously, to close the

66   *Jimi Hendrix: Voodoo Child* (Smeaton, 2010)

show by setting his guitar on fire and coaxing the flames with his hands.[67] "Everything was perfect. So I decided to destroy my guitar at the end as a sacrifice. You sacrifice the things you love. I love my guitar." [68] According to some biographers, this Festival would be Hendrix's first encounter with LSD.[69] The band toured extensively for the next two years, first with the Monkees, though this was short-lived as the young teenybopper audience often contained parents who complained that Hendrix's gyrations and raw sensuality were obscene.

The Experience released two subsequently, successful albums. It was clear Hendrix was a force to be reckoned with.

As he soared higher, Hendrix took a rather different path than I did; he remained exceptionally humble. "I don't consider myself a songwriter," he said, going on to describe his process: "A lot of times I write a lot of words all over the place on matchboxes or on napkins, and then the music makes me think of a few words I might have written." No one told him, it seems, that this *was* songwriting. Of course it was. Not to mention the fact that the songs that came out of him this way went on to become some of the most iconic songs ever written. Still, Hendrix never seemed to believe his

67   "Jimi Hendrix Bio," *Rolling Stone* editors, RollingStone.com, accessed: 05/30/2018.
68   *Jimi Hendrix: Voodoo Child* (Smeaton, 2010)
69   *Becoming Jimi Hendrix*, S. Robbie/B. Schreiber (2010)/*Jimi Hendrix: Electric Gypsy* by Harry Shapiro and Caesar Glebbeek (St. Martin's Griffin, UK: 1995)

own hype—not entirely. "I feel guilty when people say I'm the greatest guitar player on the scene. What's good or bad doesn't matter to me. What does matter is feeling and not feeling." [70]

My son and daughter both love the classics, especially blues music. They sing them for fun, and to tease them I often break into an improvised song I call, the "Beverly Hills Blues," poking fun at them for singing blues while they are financially well-off, and (as they say) "lucky." Hendrix had a notion about being able to sing the blues while rich and fortunate, and when asked about it on television, he said, "Musicians, especially young cats, they get a chance to make all this money and they say, 'Oh, this is fantastic.' They lose themselves and they forget about the music itself, you know. They forget about their talents. They forget about the other half of them. So therefore you can sing a whole lot of blues. The more money you make, the more blues you can sometimes sing." [71] Needless to say, this philosophy runs rather contrary to mine. But in Hendrix's view, losing oneself to materialism can be as much a cause for the tragic inspiration needed to sing the blues as poverty or hunger or heartbreak. And, well—who is anybody to argue with Jimi Hendrix about the blues?

The Experience split up amidst tension between Chas Chandler and a second manager, Michael Jeffrey (1933–1973), about Hendrix's desire to become more experimental with his musical endeavors. He wanted to

70   *Jimi Hendrix: Voodoo Child* (Smeaton, 2010)
71   Ibid.

experiment with jazz and ballads. "I don't want to be a clown anymore. I don't want to be a rock 'n' roll star," [72] he declared. At the same time, the public demanded the rock star, and the racial tensions of the time found Hendrix under pressure from Black Power advocates to make a stronger racial statement, and to do benefit concerts for them. "The negro riots in the States are crazy," Hendrix said, "Discrimination is crazy. I think we can live together without these problems, but because of the violence these problems aren't solved yet. I don't look at things in terms of races. I look at things in terms of people. Quite naturally, I don't like to see houses being burned." [73] Because the violence and great political unrest made him uneasy, regardless of the ethics of the cause, he found himself pulled in two directions: "I was honored, but I'm not for the aggression or violence. I just want to do what I'm doing, without getting involved in racial or political matters." [74]

The fact remained: everyone wanted a piece of Jimi.

By 1969, The Experience was over, but Hendrix was bigger than ever. It would be this year that he would play the infamous Woodstock music festival, where Hendrix would debut his album *Band of Gypsies*. This concert especially would forever cement his legacy as a live performer of extraordinary charisma and presence. This concert included the (then slightly controversial) guitar-solo rendition of the American

72   Ibid.
73   Ibid.
74   Ibid.

national anthem, which drew admiration from his younger fans and some ire from traditionalists. Still, Hendrix always seemed unflappable to those who would either criticize or praise him.

With his new band, despite his earlier stance, unrest surrounding the Vietnam War (1955–1975) seemed to move Hendrix to lean into and be less diplomatic about the political conversations of his time:

> You can always think about love, but now we're trying to give solutions to all the protests and arguments that they're having about the world today. We're trying to get the people to listen to us. Then we can say to them, "Let's go knock down the White House door." Everybody has wars within themselves and it comes out as a war against other people. You could see how desperate the whole case must be, if a kid's going to go out there and get his head busted open. *Are You Experienced* was where my head was at a couple years ago. Now, I'm into different things.[75]

There was a new album in the works with his new lineup and mission statement, but Hendrix himself would never see its release. Hendrix would die in the next year, in a gruesome fashion, suffocating on his own vomit while on barbiturates and alcohol.[76]

---

75   Ibid.
76   *The Final Days of Jimi Hendrix*, by Tony Brown (Rogan House, Ireland: 1997)

"I'm not sure I will live to be 28 years old,"
Hendrix once said. "So many beautiful things have
happened to me over the last three years. The world owes
me nothing." [77]

Hendrix's death was abrupt, it seemed, and gave
everyone a sense of whiplash. But, like most drug-related
deaths, it was only from the outside that it seemed to
come from nowhere.

In his personal life, from almost all accounts,
Hendrix was the gentlest of souls. In his own words, "I
dig anything as long as it don't hurt anybody. You're
not a loving person just because you have curly hair or
wear bells and beads. You have to believe in it, not just
throw flowers." [78] What was otherwise an almost overly
loving, caring, gentle man transformed, according to
firsthand accounts, into something entirely other under
the influence of drink. "You wouldn't expect somebody
with that kind of love to be that violent. He just couldn't
drink; he simply turned into a bastard," said his friend,
influential rock photographer, Herbie Worthington
(1944–2013). [79] According to journalist Sharon Lawrence,
Hendrix "admitted he could not handle hard liquor,
which set off a bottled-up anger, a destructive fury he
almost never displayed otherwise." [80]

There are numerous stories about Hendrix's
Jekyll-and-Hyde relationship with drinking. At the

77   *Jimi Hendrix: Voodoo Child* (Smeaton, 2010)
78   Ibid.
79   *Room Full of Mirrors: A Biography of Jimi Hendrix*, by Charles R.
Cross (Hyperion, US: 2005)
80   *Jimi Hendrix: Electric Gypsy,* by Shapiro/Glebbeek (1995)

pinnacle of the cultural wave on which Hendrix rode the crest, drugs were a central part of the culture and the message. Every fan expected this of him, and his heroes provided him drugs when they were first grooming him into a star. At the pinnacle of his success, "Few stars were as closely associated with the drug culture as Jimi." [81] And so the wheel turns, the kids influenced by drug culture become the ones who influence the next group of kids.

Hendrix's creative mind was nothing but raw potential, and I think the argument that any of that can be taken away from him and given to the substances is unfair and inaccurate, though the idea that Hendrix's genius was substance-inspired is rampant. His friends said so themselves: When he was drunk he displayed aggressive, uncharacteristic behavior he almost never displayed otherwise. The Hendrix the world fell in love with was a gentle, love-obsessed creator and musician, and this was not, by all accounts, the man he became when under the influence of alcohol. Even with other mind-altering drugs, the proof is in the pudding: Everyone else was doing the same drugs as Hendrix at the time, but nobody else sounded like Hendrix, nobody could come near him, nobody could make a guitar do what he could. The x variable here is not the drugs; it is Hendrix himself.

Still, Hendrix had a distinct philosophy about hippie culture, and the drug use that came with it, that

81   *Room Full of Mirrors,* Cross (2005)

is much more diplomatic (and surprisingly more neutral, despite his reputation) than mine. In his words:

> Although the flower scene was all tied up with sensation stuff about drugs, the "Love everybody" idea helped one hell of a lot. Of course, a lot of those hippies may get busted once in a while, but you don't hear of banks being robbed by hippies. It's your own private thing if you use drugs. Anybody should be able to think or do what they want, as long as it doesn't hurt anybody. Music is a safe type of high. It's more the way it's supposed to be. That's where highness came from anyway.[82]

To this point, even someone as staunchly anti-drug as I must say, touché. In this particular context, he is correct: drug use was as far away, at least in the popular imagination of the hippie movement, from violence as it could possibly be, which is not always the case in drug-heavy communities. My conservative and libertarian leanings seem to meet Hendrix's intuition here—common ground that a younger version of myself would never have believed existed. As long as no one gets hurt, then, ethically, his argument stands. During a press interview after Woodstock, when he was asked about drug use, Hendrix remarked, "Some people believe that they have to do this or do that to get into the music. I don't know. I have no opinions at all. Different strokes for different folks, that's all I can say." [83]

In a revealing interview in *Rolling Stone* from 1969, a year before Hendrix died, journalist Sheila Weller typifies his (and, not-so-coincidentally, two other "club" members') tumultuous relationship with the public like this:

> With Jimi Hendrix—as with Janis Joplin, Mick Jagger and Jim Morrison—mythology is particularly lavish. Unfortunately, it is often irreversible—even when it's ill-founded or after the performer has gone through changes. Several weeks ago, *Life* magazine described Jimi as "a rock demigod" and devoted several color pages to the kaleidoscopic projection of his face [...] Rock-media bedroom talk makes him King Stud of the groupies. Stories circulate that he is rude to audiences, stands up writers, hangs up photographers and doesn't talk. [84]

But, Weller concludes, "What Jimi's really about—and where his music is going—is an altogether different thing." [85] It does seem as though Hendrix is turning over a new leaf here, stating emphatically, " 'I don't want to be a clown anymore. I don't want to be a 'rock and roll star.' " [86] He is ready to be more honest and vulnerable; Weller

---

83   Ibid.
84   "Jimi Hendrix: I Don't Want To Be A Clown Anymore," by Sheila Weller, *Rolling Stone*, 09/15/1969.
85   Ibid.
86   Ibid.

describes his, "essentially fragile face and body," says he seems "boyish and vulnerable," and that he "offers questions with an unjustified fear of his own articulateness." [87]

Most prophetically of all, Weller muses, "I wonder just where he will be and what he will be doing five years from now." Unfortunately, we'll never know. The drugs got him first.

Regardless of where one stands on the drug culture or the politics of the hippie movement, Hendrix's music speaks for itself, and his seat at the top of the rock 'n' roll hierarchy is uncontroversial to this day—a fact he would have charmingly dismissed as a "distracting compliment."

---

87   Ibid.

Janis Joplin

1943 – 1970

"When you get up there
and you're playing, it's just about
letting yourself feel all those things
that you have on the inside of you
but you're trying to push them aside
because they don't make for polite
conversation. That's the only reason
that I can sing, because I first close my
eyes and let all those things that are
inside just come out."

-JANIS JOPLIN[88]

Janis Joplin

Joplin's story starts as many others do in this group—with a kid who was a little bit different, and had an early fascination with the blues. Joplin was a somewhat lonely teenager and her refuges were blues artists such as Bessie Smith (1894–1937), Otis Redding (1941–1967), Lead Belly (1988–1949),[89] folk, poetry, and painting.[90]

"She couldn't figure out how to make herself like everybody else. Thank goodness," [91] said her childhood friend Karleen Bennett in Amy Berg's documentary *Janis Joplin: Little Girl Blue* (which is probably the definitive documentary on Joplin, the only one that cuts so deep,

89   "Janis Joplin," Biography.com, accessed: 05/30/2018.
90   "Janis Joplin Bio," *Rolling Stone* editors, RollingStone.com. accessed: 05/30/2018.
91   *Janis Joplin: Little Girl Blue* (US, 2015), dir. Amy Berg, prod. Disarming Films, 103 min.

and with such incredible primary sources, putting Joplin's story in her own words in the form of family letters granted by her family's estate).[92]

She sang in church choir, where she was kicked out for not singing in a formal or traditional style. She preferred to do things her own way.

She kept a scrapbook of sketches, many of which contain silhouetted approximations of beautiful women; one of which is a sketch of a woman's face that reads, "This is a pretty girl." She was aware, in her way, that she did not quite fit the archetype of beauty that she saw in magazines, held up as the standard of the female form. She was outside the plan, the pattern, in almost every way.

"Janis was the first person to find that out that if you go rocking the boat, you might get noticed," said Michael Joplin, her younger brother, "and she rocked the boat as often as she could. She liked rocking the boat."[93]

She grew up in Port Arthur, Texas, and was, in her own description, surrounded by the hard, severe, and unaccepting culture of the South. Janis stood out from the beginning, and she was bullied throughout her high school experience. The Ku Klux Klan was politically and socially active in her town, and while the country debated segregation, she would "rock the boat" by speaking out in favor of racial integration.

The stage was set for her to join the counterculture in that every part of her seemed to be quite literally counter to the culture that she grew up in.

92   Ibid.
93   Ibid.

She was a natural singer from an early age, and it was clear that she had not been kicked out of choir for lack of skill, only for lack of submission. She would borrow blues records and proceed to wow her friends with perfect imitations of soulful singers like Odetta (1930–2008).[94]

When she got older, she played in bars and clubs all around town and in Austin. "I accidentally discovered I had this incredibly loud voice, so I started singing blues, because that was always what I liked," she said. "And, you know I got in a bluegrass band, played, you know, hillbilly music in Austin for free beer." [95]

Her high school troubles bled into her later years; she was simultaneously blessed and tortured with the fact that she was an oddball, a standout, simply *different*. This difference would be the bane of her life, and her salvation—a voice and a performer like no other cannot help but attract attention, but that attention never promised to be positive or loving. Though she got attention, she never seemed to quite get the kind of love she wanted. This, to her, must have seemed like a cruel irony. Even before fame, everybody looked, but not everybody loved.

Her old bandmate from an early bluegrass band she was in, Powell St. John (b.1940), said:

> Instantly Janis became one of the boys. People just stared openmouthed. And she was not ever

94   Ibid.
95   Ibid.

accepted really, accepted by the folk community. Growing up, her peers picked on her, and bullied her. And by the time she got to Austin, by the time I knew her, she had already been profoundly hurt over and over. Every year the fraternities held a contest and people could nominate someone to be the ugliest man, and someone nominated Janis. And all these jerks voted for her. And it crushed her. Saddest thing I ever saw… To that point I had never seen Janis cry, she had a very tough exterior. But it really got her. Got her bad.[96]

This relationship—between being a remarkable talent and a perpetual outcast—seems to be a pattern on this list, but was especially so for Janis. She was the nail that stood out, and therefore got hammered down because of her gender, her looks, her overt sexuality, her views, the intensity and power of her nontraditional voice, the way she dressed, and her rebelliousness.

For her, leaving Texas was a necessary escape from old wounds, and California seemed to symbolize a sort of freedom that she could never experience at home. In San Francisco, not only would her views on segregation be welcomed by a bigger community, but she would be part of a group large enough to march in the streets, to make the news, and to protest as loud as she had protested back home, alone.

---

96   Ibid.

Jae Whittaker, her female live-in lover when she lived in San Francisco, remarked that the pain she had learned in her time in the South had followed her there, even to this new pasture where she felt more herself: "She definitely felt the blues. She emulated [blues singers] in the sense of wanting to be like them, you know, to have the pain, and that's why she drank like she did and took drugs, because that's all part of the whole picture. She definitely needed people to tell her how great she was. I think she was totally in a conflict all the time with herself, constantly. She was unhappy. She was quite unhappy. And I think on the stage it made her feel that she was somebody—that she had something to offer." [97]

This was around the time she began to experiment with drugs, like speed. Though it brought her some respite, she seemed to be destined to be a cover act in back bars and a methedrine addict until the end.

Her new friends, out of concern for her health, collected money in a hat to fund her trip back home. They could not know the no-win situation this was for her: to send her back to the conservatism she despised, or to continue on in her freedom and become a junkie.

In a letter to her then-boyfriend (a near-miss almost-marriage that ended in infidelity on his part) from back home, she reflected: "In attempting to find a semblance of a pattern in my life, I find I've gone out with great vigor every time and gotten really fucked up. I kind of wanted to find an old man and be happy, but

---

97   Ibid.

I didn't. I just [...] became a meth freak. Jesus fucking Christ. I want to be happy so fucking bad."[98]

Eventually, a friend told Janis that a new band called Big Brother and the Holding Company, based in San Francisco but doing a show around the corner in Texas, was auditioning female singers. Janis saw them play, and became instantly hooked. She told her parents she was going on a weekend trip to Austin, and promptly ran away, back to San Francisco.

David Getz (b.1940), drummer of Big Brother, remarked that Joplin's spiriting away back to the rock 'n' roll hub of San Francisco did not come without her trademark fear of failure and rejection. Having just come from a trip home, the stated purpose of which was to get clean and turn over a new leaf, "she had a lot of misgivings. She was very afraid of drugs. She said, 'I don't ever wanna see anybody shooting drugs. I can't stand to see that, because if I see that, it's just gonna take [me] out so much.'"[99]

Sam Andrew (1941–2015), guitarist of Big Brother, reflected that her fear was in some ways justified. The first time she came to San Francisco "she had this coffeehouse career [and] she almost died *that* time."[100]

Still, while playing with her new band, she found something she had never found back home—in that swamp of unhappiness she had tried to escape, and then to ignore, and then escape again. Singing, after all, had

98   Ibid.
99   Ibid.
100   Ibid.

been her only respite from her inner self-doubts—the cheer of the crowd the hard evidence of her value that she so desired. She told her parents in a letter that, "I don't think I can go back now. I feel that this has a truer feeling, true to me. I don't feel like I'm lying now." [101]

The band began embedding themselves, through music and through being in the scene, in the counterculture, meeting and hanging with beat poets, hippies, and the Grateful Dead. Joplin was apparently once romantically involved with Ron "Pigpen" McKernan (1945–1973), a founding member of the Dead, and also, sadly, in the 27 club.

Joplin felt at home among self-proclaimed freaks. "They're not dressed up," she explained to her family, referencing a picture of all of them posed together on a San Francisco porch, "They look that way all the time. Now, taken in perspective, I'm not so far out at all, eh?" [102]

Mirroring another member of the club, Jimi Hendrix, Joplin's moment in the sun was the Monterey Pop Festival, where she made waves with her wailing banshee voice and soulful performance. She stood out, especially amongst other female singers of the time— most of whom opted for the softness of Judy Collins (b.1939), with feminine, soothing melodies. Joplin was different. She belted with intensity and unhidden rasp, much more like Robert Plant (lead singer of Led Zeppelin, b.1948) than Joan Baez (b.1941), and with about as much overt sexuality (something that

101　　Ibid.
102　　Ibid.

was not entirely embraced by some members of the
blossoming feminist movement of the time.)[103] She
could scream better, louder, and more intensely than her
male counterparts that shared a bill with her, and she
would (throughout her life) often be "the only woman in
the room." [104] She would wail and scrunch up her face
and turn red, and seem entirely unconcerned with the
traditional, delicate femininity expected of her (again, for
this, she had been teased in high school, though it became
her unique strength as a performer; you can see it in the
stunned audience faces in the Monterey footage). You had
to see her live, people would say; you had to see the vessel
from which that bellowing came. Record producer Clive
Davis (b.1932), who was in attendance at Monterey, was, in
his words, "astonished" by what he saw.[105]

They played twice at the festival. The first time,
the band, in their dedication to hippie authenticity and
anti-authoritarianism, refused to sign releases. This irked
Janis, who had no problem saying that she was going to
be "a star one day," [106] that she wanted a fancy car, that
she wanted success, despite her ingrained position in the
hippie ranks which rejected materialism outright. The
band fought amongst themselves, and eventually gave in
to Joplin and the festival organizers, resulting in what is
now one of the most famous concerts ever put on film.

The acclaim of her stage presence was coupled

103   Ibid.
104   "There's More to Janis Joplin Than Tragedy," by Joshua Barajas, PBS.
com/NewsHour, 05/02/2016.
105   *Janis Joplin: Little Girl Blue* (Berg, 2015)
106   Ibid.

with the substances; it was too much a part of the culture to be any other way. She would often drink straight from a bourbon bottle on stage, to the cheers of the crowd, and would take heroin shortly after gigs. Everyone around her did it, too.

Big Brother signed with a new manager and label soon after, and released "Piece of My Heart," which catapulted the band (and, mostly, Janis) into the spotlight. Soon, she was a bigger cultural figure than her band; all the attention was on her—her charisma, her character, and that voice. She had found the feedback and the community that she had been denied her entire young life. The record went gold in only a few days.

In a tale as old as time, as her individual popularity skyrocketed, tension began to rise with the rest of the group. Articles titled "Janis Is the Magic," implying of course that the rest of the band was not "the magic," began to surface, and it was clear that everyone within and without was singling out Janis as the X factor that made their success possible (which, if we're being honest, was true).

She left the band, which had brought her back from obscurity, within a year, and her sudden isolation brought on a huge amount of pressure to prove herself on her own. In the meantime, the drugs flowed more freely than ever before, and Joplin was keenly aware that she was straddling a dangerous edge. Sam Andrew remembered, "When Janis was in Big Brother, Peter didn't do any drugs, so we kept it toned down a lot. So now she's in Kozmic Blues, so we're doing, really, a lot of drugs because Peter's not—daddy isn't there anymore, you know? So it really got out of hand; a lot of our friends were dying that year, and she said, 'It's not gonna happen to me. My people are pioneer stock. They're tough. I've got those genes, and nothing's gonna happen to me.' " [107]

Like Hendrix, Joplin would go on to play Woodstock without her original backing band, solidifying her legend and the company she was to keep. Another head on the Mount Rushmore of rock and blues had been carved.

Peggy Caserta, a friend and lover of Joplin, paints a different portrait of the drug problem: "We were both around the same age in the South with middle-class families, but I think Janis had a harder time coming through. But, on the other hand, people tend to think because of that, that she was depressed. She wasn't. It was all fun. We shot heroin for fun. And it took the edge off. We were in the midst of one of the most social phenomenons in history." [108]

This perspective was not a popular one with those that were close to her. "She told me that she was trying to kick the habit," said David Niehaus, a former serious boyfriend who met her on a beach in Brazil, labeled by many as Joplin's true "lost love":

> I held her for two and a half days while she came down. And she was a really different

107   Ibid.
108   Ibid.

person. She was much more calm. She knew she was more beautiful. She was so free. I realized that when she sang me all these songs that they were always the blues. And that's what she felt, basically, were the blues. She could feel everybody's pain. That's one of the reasons she did heroin, so she didn't have to be involved with everybody else's life. Most people are oblivious to what's going on around them but Janis couldn't block it out.[109]

These abstract problems—being highly empathic, coupled with her own inner struggle with self-worth and love—may have served as the springboard into her heroin use. But after the angst got her that first hit, Niehaus goes on to be frank about the physical reality, that even when the demons weren't rearing their ugly heads, "She was addicted to it, you know? And I got her to stop, then when I would go away, and she'd get weak, I guess, is one way to say it, and start it again. And I told her, I can't do that part, I can't put up with that, because it's killing you. It broke my heart to see it. When I said I was leaving, she said, 'Why don't you stay and become my manager?' And it was a tempting offer, but the heroin—I couldn't even begin to put up with it." [110]

When Niehaus left, Joplin was determined to get clean—partly because she knew her health was on the line, but also, perhaps, to win Niehaus back. In her letters

109   Ibid.
110   Ibid.

to her family around this time, she gushed that Niehaus had made some noise about wanting to marry her, and that Joplin had considered it for the future—a gesture meant as much to coax her family's love and approval as it was a simple reporting of events.

This word, "future," was something that put her in two minds. On the one hand, she liked the idea of being done, eventually, with it all and settling down with someone. But, in the meantime, her creative output was reaching a fever pitch with producer Paul Rothchild (1935–1995). She recorded the Kris Kristofferson/Fred Foster-penned "Me and Bobby McGee," which would go on to become one of her best-known songs and a timeless classic, showcasing the nuance her voice was capable of beyond brute power and wailing.

To those around her during this period, it looked like heroin was behind her, and it looked like she was ready to enter a new personal renaissance. Though she was drinking heavily, she was producing her best work away from the needles. Everything was, on the surface, looking up.

Her next album, *Pearl*, would be the success she had been striving for, but she would not live to see the results of her hard work. When Joplin didn't show up to a recording session, Rothchild began to worry. He instructed the road manager to retrieve her, who found Joplin in her hotel room on the floor. She had overdosed on heroin, combined with drink.[111] She died within 16

111   *Buried Alive: The Biography of Janis Joplin,* by Myra Friedman (Crown Publishing, NY: 1992)

days of Jimi Hendrix.[112] The discussion about them and Brian Jones was the first glimmers of the 27 club as some sort of artistic curse.

That curious interim period, when Joplin left California and went back to Austin and almost gave it all up—*all* of it—is worth dissecting. She moved back to Texas to try to get off amphetamines and heroin. On the surface, this seems like a good health decision, but there is something to glean, here, in her failure to get clean at that time. She not only moved back to Texas, but she also began dressing more conservatively, putting her hair up, and wearing less jewelry, probably to please the conservative expectations of her family.[113] During this phase, she took a break from the drugs, and from *everything*: the music, the clothes, and the culture that she fell in love with. She was ready to give up her new home, get married, and conform to a community she never felt comfortable in, for the sake of her search for happiness. She was ready to leave the only other thing that brought her happiness—singing, and performing in the big city—behind. In other words, in my opinion, she tried to throw the baby out with the bathwater. She felt she had to conform her whole life to a certain mold if she gave up drugs. Inevitably, her attempt at a traditional, hyper-normal life began to wear on her, and when Big Brother came into town she saw the glittering lights on

112   "Joplin's Shooting Star: 1966–1960," ThePopHistoryDig.com, accessed: 05/30/2018.
113   "Janis Joplin," Biograpy.com.

the horizon again. San Francisco came calling and with it, the music, the parties, and the drugs—seeming to her like inevitable dominoes, all related in an all-or-nothing universe. The drugs were an aspect that always came along for the ride, and it is difficult, maybe impossible, for some people to untangle them. This, in my opinion, is a tragic and all-too-common misunderstanding.

To understand Joplin, it seems, is to understand that she was someone who sought always to achieve love, to earn love from those around her, and someone who was denied love in her extreme youth. Love, and seeking evidence of reciprocated love, was the drug she was addicted to the most.

When she returned home again, this time at the pinnacle of her fame, to go to her 10-year high school reunion in 1970, she leaned entirely in the opposite direction. She held a press conference, and seemed to go out of her way to dress like a star. In a televised interview in which she announced her plans, she wore a headdress of shocking acid pink feathers and sunglasses. She wanted a reaction from the people that "laughed [her] out of class, out of town, and out of state." She wanted some sort of cathartic justice, a triumphant return, and perhaps (at long last) acceptance and love for her true, strange, colorful self. "No one was up there and saying, 'Can you believe what Janis Joplin has been able to have done?' [She] thought it could be a triumph of people being curious and applauding, and it should have been," said her sister Laura, who was in attendance.[114] This was not to be. The town was as awkward and baffled with Joplin's presence as ever. She was too powerful at that point to bully outright, but they "presented a tire to Joplin for traveling the greatest distance to the event," which must have seemed a bizarre act of passive-aggression, of deliberately ignoring the elephant in the room: Joplin had become a worldwide icon. Still, it seemed the opinion of her old town mattered to her. She was still denied—in that small but significant way—the love she craved.

Her sister Laura argues that even given this friction, she was at her core not nearly as dark and tormented as she is often portrayed. "While I think Janis did have some unhappiness in her, she was basically a very happy person who was ecstatic with her success."[115] She also argues that the taunting Joplin received in high school was no more or less than any other teenager dealt with at the time, but became a more internal problem because Joplin "let their taunts grind deeper and deeper into her psyche, until the events were elaborately woven into her personal mythology."[116] This seems to mirror Niehaus' assessment that Joplin was a highly sensitive, highly empathic person. Things that others brush off seemed to affect Joplin deeply.

In a televised interview soon after her death, John Lennon (1940–1980) remarked that he had received a

114   "There's More to Janis Joplin Than Tragedy," Barajas, PBS.com, 2016
115   Ibid.
116   Ibid.

tape in the mail that Joplin had sent him, of her singing "Happy Birthday" to him. The tape had arrived post-mortem. When asked how future overdoses like this could be prevented in the industry, Lennon said: "The basic thing nobody asked is, why do people take drugs of any sort, from alcohol to Aspros to hard drugs? I mean, is there something wrong with a society that's making us so pressurized that we cannot live in it without guarding ourselves against it?" [117]

"I managed to pass my 27th birthday without really feeling it," Joplin writes, in a letter to her family, unknowingly very near the end. "Two years ago I didn't even wanna be it. No, that's not true. I've been looking around, and I've noticed something. After you reach a certain level of talent, and quite a few have that talent, the deciding factor's ambition. Or as I see it, how much you really need—need to be loved, and need to be proud of yourself. And I guess that's what ambition is. It's not all depraved quests for position or money. Maybe it's for love, lots of love." [118]

Perhaps the two quotes above, taken together, reveal a partial answer to what was wrong with society as Joplin saw it: a simple lack of love.

In her interview with *Vogue*, Amy Berg (director of *Janis Joplin: Little Girl Blue*) wished to debunk some of the "tragic" clichés that attached themselves to Joplin's story:

I don't want to minimize the fact that she was

---

117   *Janis Joplin: Little Girl Blue* (Berg, 2015)
118   Ibid.

drinking all the time and doing drugs. That, ultimately, did take her away from us. But I do feel that women are remembered differently than men in that realm of young stars who overdosed. Men are remembered for who they were; women are remembered for the tragedy, the loss. I wanted to put some breath in that. As tragic as the loss is, [I wanted to show] what her life was like, what she gave up… I think she would want to be remembered for being beautiful and talented and passionate. She was only 27 years old. She was just learning lessons in life. She was still so young.[119]

---

119   "The New Janis Joplin Documentary Is a Portrait of the Artist as a Very Young Woman," by Julia Felstenhal, Vogue.com, 11/24/2015.

Jim Morrison

1943 – 1971

"People talk about how great
love is, but that's bullshit.
Love hurts. Feelings are disturbing.
People are taught that pain is evil
and dangerous. How can they
deal with love if they're afraid to feel?
Pain is meant to wake us up.
Pain is a feeling—your feelings are a
part of you. You should stand up for
your right to feel your pain."

—JIM MORRISON[120]

120   "Jim Morrison: Ten Years Gone," by Lizze James, *Creem* magazine,
1981.

Jim
Morrison

If Brian Jones was the first to get people talking about the 27 club, Jim Morrison was probably the figure that solidified it as the subject of an urban myth. There is almost no musician on this list more shrouded in a strange kind of mythology than Morrison. One need only watch the opening scenes of the 2009 documentary *When You're Strange*, in which a hitchhiking Morrison listens to a radio broadcast reporting the details of his own real-life death, to realize that the Doors' fanbase, and the cult of Morrison, are not your ordinary fan communities. There is a certain magical thinking fans are willing to grant when talking about Morrison, and this quasi-religious fixation is something he consciously courted during his life with the Doors.

I must have first heard about the Doors around

1966, when I was 15 years old. I heard "Light My Fire," of course. I must have dismissed it as a jazz record at first; it was just so out of the box. The Doors were so different, they couldn't help but be an acquired taste. But when Jim Morrison started doing outlandish things on stage, I started to be keenly observant of the band.

His look—that all-important factor that artists are loath to talk about—was impossible to ignore. When those classic black-and-white photos came out of Morrison looking like the statue of David, it was clear that all eyes would be on him, no matter who he pissed off.

And like John Lennon before him, there was the sense that Morrison had a deeper soul than all the rest. He was different. He was well-read. He loved poetry. He was literate. He wasn't just a rock 'n' roll vagabond. The "Lizard King" persona, like Bowie's "Ziggy Stardust" or "Aladdin Sane," established a duel-identity phenomenon, with larger-than-life myths; the lyrics dealt with all sorts of eclectic and even ethereal subject matter. Unlike most bands, Morrison's least well-known lyrics dealt with simple sex and the usual fare; that was merely a moody backdrop to something else he was aiming for.

Photos, stories, and film footage seemed to suggest that this was a guy who had his inner demons. What they were, where they came from, or why they manifested in him, was a mystery to me at the time—perhaps more so than all the rest on this list. He was simply fascinating, but it was hard to dissect what troubled someone who truly seemed to have it all.

It didn't hurt that he and his band had a unique,

singular point of view regarding their approach to their songs and their sound. No one had ever sounded like the Doors. And no one has since.

Bing Crosby (1903–1977), Elvis Presley (1935–1977), and Frank Sinatra (1915–1998) were his greatest vocal influences. He had little to no actual musical ability; he fancied himself a poet, first. He was just...different.

The unlikely son of Rear Admiral George Morrison, who would later become "the commander of U.S. Naval forces [...] during the Gulf of Tonkin Incident," [121] Morrison was hardly the ideal army brat. He would grow up, after all, to be the singer of prominent anti-Vietnam protest songs—a central figure in the rift between generations, between culture and counterculture. But when he was a child, he constantly moved with his family to various naval bases, as was necessary for his father's job.

He was, paradoxically, a dutiful student and a troublemaker, with a high IQ and aptitude for academics, but also a rebellious streak that caused him to be a minor terror to his teachers. Here, we see glimmers of the pattern established by Brian Jones: Morrison discovered drink almost as early as he discovered William Blake and Friedrich Nietzsche. He made the Dean's list, but apparently only stayed in school to dodge the draft.

He attended UCLA film school, with one art film to his name from his time there. At that point, he was

121   "Jim Morrison," Biography.com, accessed: 05/30/2018.

already taking LSD with future bandmate Ray Manzarek (1939–2013) "several times a month," [122] waxing philosophic about psychedelia, filmmaking, blues, and jazz. He eventually received a bachelor's degree in film, though he did not attend his own graduation, and lived aimlessly afterwards, at one point living on a friend's rooftop in California.

As the relatively well-known story goes, he met Manzarek on Venice beach by chance, and remembered him from college. In Manzarek's description of this reunion in his book, he describes the intangible charisma that affected not only Morrison's later fans, but even those that were closest to him pre-stardom: "The sun is streaming in behind him. I see this silhouetted figure walking along in the shallows, kicking up water. He's like an Indian deity, like Krishna—the Blue God—in semi-silhouette, wearing cutoffs, without a shirt, weighing about 135 pounds. Thin, about six feet tall; rail-thin kind of guy with long hair. There was something strangely familiar about this watery apparition. Was this a manifestation of the ocean itself? Did our mother conjure up this solidity? Or was this a projection of my own Jungian inclinations toward liquidity and wholeness? I looked again, with more intensity, and who should emerge from the light, from behind the sun, into my field of vision, into my field of consciousness, but Jim Morrison!" [123] Clearly, there was

---

122   *The Doors: When You're Strange* (US, 2009), dir. Tom DiCallo, dist. Rhino Entertainment, 86 min.
123   *Light My Fire: My Life With The Doors*, by Ray Manzarek (Berkley, US: 1999)

something about Jim, even before the band, that inspired a sort of cultish devotion from people around him, even people who knew him well.

Morrison sang him a poem he had written, "Moonlight Drive," *a cappella* on the spot, which eventually became a well-loved Doors song. Manzarek was moved by the poetic lyrics, and in that moment, they decided to form a band.

Jim left his rooftop squalor and moved in with Manzarek and his then-girlfriend. Guitarist Robby Krieger (b.1946) and percussionist John Densmore (b.1944) followed, and the band shared interests in transgressive poetry, philosophy, and psychedelia, which they partook in together, often taking impromptu sojourns into the California desert together for drug trips. Morrison particularly had an obsession with Aldous Huxley and William Blake, thus they decided to name their band, "the Doors" after Aldous Huxley's book about the deeper meaning of mescaline drug trips, *The Doors Of Perception* (itself named after a line in a William Blake poem). At the time of the band's founding, Morrison had never actually sung in any capacity besides to himself, and Krieger was a brand new convert to electric guitar. Not to be deterred, Manzarek rented a house to serve as their home base for writing and rehearsing.

"Jim did not play an instrument," Manzarek recalls, "He heard songs in his head and would sing them with his lyrics, then John, Robby, and I would create the melody, the arrangement, the chord changes, and the rhythm. We would create the music of the Doors around him." [124]

Morrison suggested that they all write songs for the band, but Krieger was apparently the only one who brought a song to the table. It was "Light My Fire." [125]

By that point, the entire band were all seasoned veterans of psychedelics and alcohol. It was, simply, a part of the rising culture. It was also likely a part of Morrison's rebellion against his strict, conservative, military upbringing. There was no version of Morrison's story that makes sense without drug and drink, it seems. His heroes were all the "dangerous drunks" of the literary and film worlds. The framework of his intellectual idols like Huxley were laid out plainly. None of them abstained from dangerous living and pursuing philosophy through substances, and neither would young Morrison.[126] The philosophy of the Doors' namesake quote seemed, to them, to be less a branding move and more a creed that they were determined to follow: "If the doors of perception were cleansed every thing would appear to man as it is, Infinite. For man has closed himself up, till he sees all things thro' narrow chinks of his cavern." [127] The meaning of this, of course, is essential to the worldview of the counterculture/hippie movement that we are all now familiar with. That is, that

124   "The Doors' Manzarek, Guest Guitarist Marc Benno Remember Jim Morrison," by Chris M. Junior, Goldmine.com, 10/26/2011.
125   *The Doors: When You're Strange* (DiCallo, 2009)
126   "Jim Morrison Bio," RollingStone.com.
127   *The Doors of Perception and Heaven and Hell*, by Aldous Huxley (Chatto & Windus, UK: 1954)

psychedelic drugs do not distort our perception of reality, they actually present a *more accurate* version of reality— an infinitely abstract one. This would mean of course that the "narrow chinks of [our] cavern" represent the normal reality most of us live in. How sincere anyone who subscribed to this worldview really was about penetrating into the deep mysteries of the universe (as opposed to using mystical language as an excuse to get high because they, simply, wanted to get high) can be debated on a case-by-case basis. But with Morrison and the Doors, there was a sense that they really were serious about their convictions. Drugs were not just recreation, in their view, as they were for many on this list. Drugs were the answer, the pathway to something profound and valuable, or so Morrison and the group claimed.

The Doors subsisted on self-recorded demos for a time, and after a few early gigs they were spotted by the female talent booker at the Whisky a Go Go, who immediately "fell for Morrison." [128] They were hired soon after to play as the house band of the Whisky. Far from the casual venue it is now, the Whisky was once the hot spot of all hot spots in Los Angeles, featuring the trademark "Go-Go dancers" of its name on a raised platform above the stage and hosting the biggest acts of the time. The Doors, virtually unknown at that point, would go on to open for Van Morrison (b.1945) and rock band Buffalo Springfield.

They gained a reputation due to Morrison's

128   *The Doors: When You're Strange* (DiCallo, 2009)

unusual but fascinating stage presence. In the beginning, perhaps out of nervousness or inexperience, he would occasionally stand with his back to the crowd, never showing his face. Other times, he would launch into strange convulsions without warning, improvise lyrics, and wail drunkenly, to the delight of the audience. His very unpredictability seemed to be a major draw.

As their local popularity grew, a heavily acid-dosed Morrison launched into a particularly explicit version of "The End." While they play the song, Morrison improvised a version of the lyrics, including the now-famous Oedipus-inspired lyrics about killing his father and raping his mother, without warning any of his bandmates. The Doors were fired, but their momentum was already sealed, and they were soon signed to Elektra Records, where they recorded their first album with Paul Rothchild.

Their first single, "Break On Through," did not even break the top 100. However, the Krieger-penned "Light My Fire," the first song he had written in his life, hit a nerve with the public, and landed at number one.[129]

Morrison did not keep in touch with his family and did not inform them of the news. A family friend bought the album and showed Jim's brother, remarking that the "guy on the cover looked a little like Jim." Once his parents and brother realized it was actually him, the revelation was further complicated by Jim's description of his family inside the album's sleeve: "Family Info: Dead." [130]

129   Ibid.
130   Ibid.

Breaking into the mainstream did nothing to tame Morrison, and indeed he seemed to enjoy the idea that he was an avatar for the counterculture, for drug culture, and for everything taboo. Their songs began to chart, and they seemed to become famous overnight.

The group was banned from the Ed Sullivan Show after infamously agreeing to, and then neglecting to, change a reference to getting high in one of their lyrics, which Morrison then sang live on-air. The event at Whisky, it seemed, foreshadowed a frontman with a disdain for all authority, who could not, and would not, be reigned in by anyone, any rule, or any social more. Those who attempted to enforce censorship and restrictions on Morrison did not realize that he fed on their outrage, and that their fan base would only love him more for it.

Morrison's behavior from then on was either that of a calculated provocateur, a raving narcissistic drunkard, or some combination of the two. His concerts, much like the early Rolling Stones shows, often included interruptions by police officers for the riotous, aggressive, and transgressive energy he encouraged. He was simultaneously high- and low-brow, courting the character of highfalutin poet one moment and an inebriated, hedonistic degenerate the next. Morrison seemed, as time went on, to relish confrontations with police. In one instance, when a cop ordered him out of the backstage area (failing to recognize him), Morrison responded with a swift, "go fuck yourself," instead of correcting the officer's mistake. The officer, apparently enraged, maced Morrison in the face. Morrison took to the stage shortly after, describing the encounter and taunting the policeman, trying to get him to speak into the microphone. Instead, the police in attendance arrested Morrison for "disturbing the peace."

Much like the Stones, Morrison's confrontations with the law fueled his fans' frenzied attraction to him and his bad-boy persona. The more trouble that Morrison got into, the more they loved him for it. People came to shows as much to see the music as to see what the "madman" may do next. He seemed to love attention, and love stimulating and provoking people. He would sometimes walk into his own crowds before concerts so that people could grope and fondle him, encouraging as much madness and transgression in others as they expected of him.[131]

During one infamous occasion on March 1st, 1969, in Miami, after a long and frustrated rant, Morrison allegedly exposed his genitals and simulated masturbation to the crowd. This event inspired decency rallies and outcrying articles across the nation, and Morrison eventually had to turn himself into the FBI. He was convicted of a felony charge, and was sentenced to hard labor.[132]

In 2010, Morrison was actually pardoned of this offence by Florida's Clemency Board. Doors drummer John Densmore was in favor of this move, saying that the incident never even happened. He said to *The Hollywood*

131   Ibid.
132   Ibid.

Reporter that year:

> Can I just make a statement? He didn't
> do it! I was there; if Jim had revealed the golden
> shaft, I would have known. There were hundreds
> of photographs taken and a ton of cops and
> no evidence. Yeah, Jim was a drunk and a
> sensational, crazy guy, but he was also a great
> artist and I want him to be remembered for the
> art as well as the craziness.[133]

Onstage, all of these rumors and antics nevertheless served him well. Off-stage, he gained a reputation as a mean drunk, and an unpredictable entity. Stories spread of his spats around Los Angeles, his conflicts with the cops, and an encounter with Janis Joplin where Morrison was apparently so intolerable, burying his face in her lap without consent, that she hit him over the head with a bottle.[134] He was rewarded for things like this onstage, after all, how could it not bleed over into life itself?

Up until *Waiting For the Sun*, Morrison's antics were apparently all well-placed, and fed the legend. "I'd say 75 percent or 80 percent of the time, he was right there. He was very professional in the studio," Manzarek remembered. "This legendary maniac was very, very

133   "The Doors' John Densmore: Jim Morrison 'Didn't' Expose Himself," by Shirley Halperin, HollywoodReporter.com, 12/02/2010.
134   *Long Time Gone: The Autobiography of David Crosby*, by David Crosby and Carl Gottlieb (Da Capo Press, US: 2005)

good in the studio." [135]

This professionalism, unfortunately, was not to last. Morrison began to come into his vocal sessions severely intoxicated, leaving Krieger to take up writing approximately half the songs on their upcoming album, *The Soft Parade*. This would mark the first time Krieger and Morrison would specify in the liner notes who wrote what song, where before Jim insisted the credits simply read, "The Doors." [136] If the Stones' pattern can be seen as a foreshadowing, the next part of Morrison's story becomes predictable. While Manzarek tried to slow down his own psychedelic use, turning his attention more toward meditation for his reality-transcending mission, Morrison dug his heels in, and his apparent alcoholism and erratic behavior were beginning to take a toll. Morrison would pass out in the middle, or sometimes at the beginning, of concerts. Manzarek would have to take over and sing Jim's vocal parts (in his own impressive baritone) just to keep the concert going.

Morrison, with encouragement from his on-again-off-again girlfriend Pamela Courson, announced that he wanted to pursue poetry, and quit the band. The band pleaded with Morrison to give it more time, and to get sober. Morrison obliged for only a week, until he came crashing down yet again.

After going on a long drinking binge in London, Morrison discovered that the rest of the band had allowed a car company to use "Light My Fire" in a

---

135   "The Doors' Manzarek," Junior, Goldmine.com, 2011.
136   *The Doors: When You're Strange* (DiCallo 2009)

commercial, which infuriated Morrison; commercials, to him, were too much of a crass, materialistic symbol to be associated with what he deemed sacred. This, and Morrison's near-constant drinking, began to separate him from his once close comrades. As the venues grew, Morrison became distant, at times ranting to crowds incomprehensibly, encouraging riots, and swearing at his own fans.

Near the end of his life, Morrison visibly gained weight. He was "deeply affected by the deaths of Hendrix and Joplin...[joking] to friends, 'They're looking at number three.'" [137] Everyone in Morrison's world was disturbed by the incoming President Nixon, the Manson murders, and a palpable sense that the Love Generation's LSD-inspired utopian dream was dying. [138] Morrison hid behind a philosopher's beard, alcohol, and cocaine in those later days, and became more reclusive. The band's tour and recording schedule was affected by the various criminal charges against Morrison—once again mirroring the difficulties of Brian Jones.

After recording the acclaimed, bluesier *LA Woman* album, Morrison moved to Paris with Pamela Courson, to focus on poetry, never to return.

The cause of Morrison's death is disputed. Jim Ladd on the long-running rock radio station 95.5 remarked that a "cloud of mystery hangs over Morrison's death. Some claim he's still alive and that his death was just a hoax, perhaps planned by Morrison himself.

137   Ibid.
138   Ibid.

Numerous sightings of the singer have already been reported." [139] Morrison, very likely, would have enjoyed these stories, as they recall the conspiracy theories surrounding one of his heroes, Elvis Presley. *Rolling Stone* simply described it as "heart failure." [140] The fact that the details of his death remain murky, of course, only add to his mythic status among fans; some conspiracy theorists to this day insisting he never died at all, but in fact escaped to seclusion in some foreign country. He was buried in Paris in the "poet's corner" of Père Lachaise Cemetery, near many of his favorite poets and authors. His gravesite became a hippie pilgrimage, so much so that the stylized bust of his head and shoulders was damaged to the point of having to be removed from the site.

Morrison is a difficult character to separate from his substance abuse. There was a philosophy involved in his use of psychedelics that was grafted into the movement he was advocating. It is the reason many people begin to follow the Doors, this counterculture that is inexorably tangled up with changing the state of the brain with substances. For my part, it is more my curiosity that makes me want to extradite his drug use from the rest of him. Without judgment, I want to know how much of it was the drink, how much of it was the drugs, and how much was Morrison himself. He had an abnormally high IQ, how much was on purpose, and therefore inimitable? How much of his stage presence, his toying with the expectations of the crowd, was mere

139   Ibid.
140   "Jim Morrison Bio," RollingStone.com.

drunken accident? This latter question is hard to answer, and I think it's a shame that so much of his legend might just be due to intoxication, the flashing of flesh, the rock star antics mixed with good looks, as opposed to the lyrics, the poetry, and the songwriting, which could only have come from a singular intellect. I am convinced that one cannot stumble haphazardly into poetry and abstract thinking, but you can certainly stumble into rock stardom, with the right look, the right time, the right place, the right confidence (I should know). With Morrison, it is genius versus mere drunken tabloid fodder, and it is sometimes difficult to separate the wheat from the chaff in that regard. Still, though it may be blasphemous amongst Doors fans to say, I am sad that I never got to see what else he had. That high intellect undoubtedly had more to offer, and whether or not the drugs and drink helped or limited him in his pursuits is something that I believe remains more ambiguous than drug enthusiasts like to admit. A Morrison who eventually got sober, I suspect, would still have much music and poetry to write, much to say about people, society, and the world, whether one agrees with his point of view or not. But, that's just one musician's opinion.

My son, who has jammed with Doors guitarist Robby Krieger on a number of occasions for fun and for charitable events, called him to get his point of view and to reflect:

> Jim Morrison was a genius, and I think if
> he hadn't been schizophrenic, he still would be a

genius. His brother and sister are totally normal people, they all have the same parents. People say, "Oh, Jim hated his dad because he was an Admiral," and all that. But, I don't really buy that anger is any reason why someone makes good music. Although Jim definitely did have an Oedipus complex. It was a lot more obvious than most people think. I mean everybody has an Oedipus complex I guess, guys do anyway, they love their mother and hate their father symbolically, but with Jim it was literal. He literally loved his mother, I mean he would take acid and see his mother's face in the moon. His dad was the big Navy guy, you know, and he used to take Jim out on the boat and, y'know, make him shoot guns and stuff. Jim hated that. So, y'know, when you say "kill your father," what they really mean is that you want to do better, be bigger than your father. You want to be able to do something that outshines your father. But with Jim—hey, who knows.

Back when Jim passed away, and Janis and Jimi, it was kind of "the style." People thought, "Gee, maybe that's the time to go, you know, when you're at your best." Then you don't have to get old, and, y'know, people forget how magic it was. I don't really go along with that especially. To me, I really don't think Jim had that in mind If Jim were still here, I don't even know if he'd still be doing music. I know he would be into films. That's really what he wanted to do, direct films. He kind of got sidetracked, I think. He went to film school. But I know he'd be doing something sooner or later. He didn't plan to go out like that, I'm sure. I don't know about Janis, and Jimi…I mean, hell, in those days everybody was into the fuckin' heroin. You know? That was just popular. And nobody at the time really realized that you can't just do that drug and drink at the same time. I think we lost a lot of people that way.

To the kids who romanticize this stuff, I would say that it's a waste to die early, because a lot of people don't even accomplish anything really good until they get to be 50 years old or more. A lot of times people think, Jimi and Janis and Jim are up there jammin' out and they're still 27 years old. Kind of makes you think, what if when you go to heaven or whatever, you stay the age that you died at? I would hate to be 80 for the rest of eternity, so I guess that's why that's attractive. But I don't think it works that way.

Jean-Michel Basquiat

1960 – 1988

"I don't listen to what art critics say. I don't know anybody who needs a critic to find out what art is."

–JEAN-MICHEL BASQUIAT[141]

Jean-Michel Basquiat

To the uninitiated, much like Robert Johnson, Jean-Michel Basquiat's work seems to be almost childlike in its simplicity. This is not necessarily unintentional; Basquiat would deliberately paint and draw with a straightforward, energetic style, utilizing words, phrases, and names that were written numerous times and scribbled out, even going so far as to sometimes hold his instruments the way a child would.[142] "I want to make paintings that look as if they were made by a child,"[143] he remarked to close friend Fred Brathwaite (b.1959), also known as rapper and artist Fab 5 Freddy.

142   *Jean-Michel Basquiat: The Radiant Child* (US, 2010), dir. Tamra Davis, prod. Arthouse Films, 88 min.
143   "Burning Out," by Anthony Haden-Guest, VanityFair.com, 04/02/2014.

However, this first-glance aesthetic belies the sheer breadth and depth of the historical, cultural, and personal allusions contained in each painting, indicating a highly educated and eclectic artist. There are riddles drawn over riddles, bobbing close to the surface of every piece if one only cares to look more closely. Basquiat's art would feature references to the pantheon of canon artists like Da Vinci and Van Gogh all the way to blues and jazz artists like Robert Johnson and John Coltrane, the father of evolutionary biology Charles Darwin, Wolfgang Mozart, and many more. It seemed there was no academic or artistic area that didn't hold some value to this 19, 20, 21-year-old artist. Some would say these references began as a way to prove his place among this pantheon of household names—and the critics and fans, eventually, would come to agree that he deserved to be there.

Basquiat was born in Brooklyn, and his mother exposed him to art at the Brooklyn Museum from a very early age. His father was an accountant—a well-off, conservative man in suits and ties, as will become a pattern on this list, along with Morrison and Cobain. The wild ones simultaneously rebel and seek attention from their conservative father figures. "He craved parental approval," [144] remarked a school friend, and pining for a better relationship with his father would be a constant source of frustration and longing throughout the artist's short life.

The young Basquiat was hit by a car as a child

144   Ibid.

and had to have his spleen removed, a moment that would become formative in his development. During his recovery time, his mother would bring him things to read, including a copy of *Gray's Anatomy*. The illustrations (and even text captions and technical jargon) inside would become a major artistic influence for him; anatomical and medical motifs are found in many of his later paintings.[145]

Basquiat's home life was less than ideal. "He would complain about his father being violent, and his mother was in and out of institutions due to mental illness,"[146] said his childhood friend and early collaborator Al Diaz.

One persistent myth about his home life, however, is that he grew up in total urban squalor. This, undoubtedly, comes from certain preconceptions about what the background of a "graffiti artist" must be, and perhaps also by certain notions that Basquiat would spread himself. His father would remark that, "Jean-Michel, for some reason, liked to give the impression that he grew up in the ghetto. I was driving a Mercedes-Benz."[147]

In addition, Basquiat's vast breadth of education was, especially during his time, overlooked by critics and casual fans. "Some people might not know that Basquiat

---

145   "American Graffiti: Memories of Jean-Michel Basquiat," by Hayley Maitland, Vogue.co.uk, 09/20/2017.
146   Ibid.
147   "Burning Out," Haden-Guest, VanityFair.com, 2014.

came from a very cultured background," said art curator Eleanor Nairne. "His father was an accountant from Haiti and his mother was second-generation Puerto Rican. He was exposed to an incredible amount of art and exhibitions. He also attended the private school St. Anne's, and then later the progressive City-As-School. So he had a very educated background, even though he dropped out of school at a relatively young age." [148]

The stereotype of the graffiti artist as street dweller only became partly accurate when, at 17, Basquiat ran away from home, and relied on couch-surfing, staying with girlfriends like Suzanne Mallouk (later his muse), and getting by whichever way he could. "I was determined not to go home again," he said. "I thought I was going to be a bum forever." [149] He had, quite literally, no money at the time, which did little to deter his ambition of living in Manhattan. He would sneak onto subways to get around, and this hardship was apparently understood as a consequence of the community he chose. There was a romanticism to roughing it and being broke, for Basquiat. "You just end up surviving when you have to, I guess," he said. "I used to look for money at the Mudd Club on the floor." [150]

It was in New York that Basquiat found himself among the "Downtown 500," a community of an estimated 500 or so of hard-partying Manhattan artists

148   "Debunking Basquiat's Myths: Curator Eleanor Nairne on What We Get Wrong About the Misunderstood Artist," by Lorena Muñoz-Alonso, Artnet. com, 09/18/2017.
149   *Jean-Michel Basquiat: The Radiant Child* (Davis, 2010)
150   Ibid.

of various kinds (music, visual, literary) based around the Bowery, all making a living, or trying to, solely with their art. The concept of a plan B, or a day job, was abandoned in favor of a romantic, all-or-nothing creative lifestyle, and this caused a community of "cool kids" to form, who in turn attracted a varied mix of party-goers, from the most destitute starving artists to celebrities like Debbie Harry. It was a magical time in New York for these youngsters, a time when young, broke artists could actually afford (give or take) to scrape by in Manhattan without proper 9-to-5s.

It was then that the name "SAMO" started to appear, tagged on brick walls, under overpasses, and on subways. The Downtown 500 would talk about this reclusive graffiti artist, SAMO (which stood for "same old shit"), the way we tend to talk about Banksy today—a sort of street visionary that elevates the urban tagging tradition into something more interesting. It was Jean-Michel and Al Diaz that were marking the rising community with their bold statements. Brathwaite, in the documentary *The Radiant Child*, remarked, "The whole objective in doing graffiti is fame. Achieving a certain status and a certain recognition. Like, I'm going to take control of that space and people are gonna know me." [151] The ambitious young Basquiat apparently concurred with this goal.

The SAMO tags were odd for graffiti, especially at their time, because they did not take the form that,

---

151   Ibid.

even now, stands as the sort of classic archetype for tagging: a name (or more commonly, a nickname/ street name) of the tagger in some sort of stylized or balloon-lettered font... In other words, a mere ego-driven, territorial gesture. SAMO was this, but also more, and would include strange expressions, musings, and quotables. As described by Glenn O'Brien: "The SAMO tags had content. They were like poetry."

Basquiat eventually revealed his identity as SAMO on public-access television and at various legendary parties with the Downtown 500.

His first foray into selling his art was when he was forced (by the mere cost of living) to start making t-shirts and postcards with his art printed on them. "The first paintings I made were on windows I found on the street and on doors I found on the street," [152] he recalled. He would even paint on his girlfriend's refrigerator door. It was not uncommon to find Basquiat standing on the street wearing paint-splattered clothing, offering postcards and t-shirts to the next passerby, at one point walking into a restaurant where Andy Warhol was dining and offering his wares. Warhol actually bought a few postcards, marking Basquiat's first glint of artistic validation.

Though he struggled financially, he found himself among the epicenter of the culture and music of his time, and this was the strange dichotomy considered normal for the Downtown 500—and the scene was

---

152   Ibid.

growing, pushing up against the art world establishment.

"He was a star when he was broke," [153] said Glenn O'Brien, who would be among the first to give him money so that he could produce, and would later introduce him to Debbie Harry, who bought his very first on-canvas painting.

One of Basquiat's first curators, Diego Cortez (b.1946), started his own show called PS1, and this was the show that tipped Basquiat's ball into the net. "I was just tired of seeing white walls, with white people, with white wine, you know?" Cortez remarked, and this sentiment seemed to be a shared one, one that was brewing in the new wave of rebellious, bohemian, couch-surfing artists of Manhattan. It seemed to be the right place and the right time for an artist like Basquiat.

People lined around the block to get into the show, and Diego Cortez remarked that everyone who saw Basquiat's work was immediately interested in it.

After he proved himself at PS1, legendary gallerist Annina Nosei granted him studio space in her gallery in SoHo, where he was also given money for canvases and materials. It was there that his productivity soared, with access to traditional materials and a studio, which seemed to make his work more and more difficult for the establishment art world to either ignore or to condemn him to the mere "street art" niche. Nosei gave him his first solo exhibition, the first with his name advertised in the newspaper. Everything he made, apparently, sold out

153   Ibid.

in a single night, and he made six figures in 24 hours.

Nosei would help him sell his pieces in Europe, where he made over 100,000 dollars in cash right away, a sum of money that proved difficult to transport across international borders. "The police caught us, and refused to believe that the African-American man whose luggage consisted of a few boxes tied with heavy rope had made that amount from his paintings instead of drugs. It took several emergency calls to Emilio [Mazzoli, art dealer] before the misunderstanding was cleared up." [154]

Once he was in demand, his rise was meteoric, and all the while this stoked his ambitious and competitive fires. He would frame his ascent in the art world in sports metaphors, often referencing a "boxing match" with the current artist *en vogue* at the moment.

He began to exhibit all over the world, just as he turned 21. By this point, he had become a millionaire in a single year, and his paintings were being ravenously purchased by all manner of collectors.

A now-iconic image of him depicts him painting in a splattered and stained, brand-new Armani suit, similar to a suit he wore on the cover of the *New York Times*. This image represents his two minds regarding money and material. True worldwide fame and fortune had found him, or he them, and afterwards, followed constant attention, money, dating celebrities (like Madonna), and features on runway fashion shows. He was art's rock star overnight. However, even though fame

154 "American Graffiti," Maitland, Vogue.co.uk, 2017.

was his goal, and he was ambitious, he still maintained a strong sense of social justice and a disdain for the establishment. In the words of his girlfriend Suzanne Mallouk:

> For Jean-Michel, money was a weapon—a tool that he could use to expose people's hypocrisies and racism. We would take limousines everywhere as a sort of parody of the hip hop stars like Run-D.M.C. who did the same. Occasionally, he would drop $100 bills out of the window for the homeless people outside. Once, we were at dinner at a fancy Italian restaurant called Barbetta, and a group of Wall Street bankers started laughing and pointing at us, asking, "How can you afford to be here? Are you a pimp? Is that your whore?" Jean-Michel kept quiet, called over the waiter, and paid for their dinner. It must have cost thousands of dollars. When one of them sheepishly came over to thank him afterwards, he just slapped another $500 in his hand and said: "Sorry, I forgot the tip." [155]

When he met Andy Warhol again, Warhol snapped a Polaroid of him and created a piece with the photo, and Basquiat in turn painted his and Andy's faces in a close, stylized approximation of the Polaroid itself, with Warhol astounded by the speed at which he

[155]   Ibid.

produced. It was a strange, quick exchange of two artists at the center of the public eye, and would mark the true beginning of their very public artistic relationship.

Basquiat seemed conscious of the fact that his close friendship with Andy was as much a career trophy as it was a genuine relationship, but there was no denying the deep, shared affection they had for each other from the get-go.

This was the scene that frequented the infamous Studio 54, which is a name that needs little introduction. Warhol was a fixture there, as was anyone who was anyone at the time. I was there often enough, and ran into both gentleman on various occasions. I had more contact with Andy, sadly, than I ever had with Jean-Michel. When I went to 54, Andy would come over and say a few words, and then slink back into the shadows. He would never dress as outrageously as the others, as I remember. A conservative, casual suit, belying his centrality to the counterculture. And that trademark hair. No matter who I had on my arm, Andy liked to watch; he seemed to like to watch people in general. He liked to watch who was coming, who was going, who was doing what and to whom. Despite all the craziness in 54—the loud music, hydraulic lifts picking people up off the ground, riding glittery stars like horses above everyone's heads, people of all sexual persuasions flirting and touching and more, everyone having a great time—Andy always struck me as perhaps a lonely person. In the middle of all the commotion, Andy would be sitting at a table, with a few scene makers and just...watch.

Not in a judgmental way, not in a voyeuristic way. He was, it always seemed to me, a sweet, innocent man. No matter what was going on at 54, I often found myself looking over at Andy. In all our interactions, I found him to regard me as though he were looking at an art piece, which was the same way he looked at everyone. It seemed that Andy collected people, in a way, and once Basquiat came on the scene, Andy became utterly fascinated, fixated on him.

Basquiat seemed to have a disdain for the minimalism movement that was *en vogue* at the time, a style of art I myself cannot stand: pure white or black canvases with nothing on them, a simple box on the floor, things like that. Boring, sterile, medical. This pretentious world did not accept Basquiat and relegated him to a partitioned, separate subgenre. He tried to donate a massive piece to MoMA and the Whitney, and they replied that he wasn't "worth the space." Herb and Lenore Scharr, two early collectors who had a close relationship with Basquiat, remarked:

> He was a genius who broke with the traditions of the past, and curators struggled to fit him into their narrative of art history. About six months before he died, he told us that he wanted to see his paintings in a major New York gallery. We said we would donate some of our works to the Museum of Modern Art and the Whitney. Both turned us down. No

interest. After Jean-Michel died, of course, both rushed to purchase his work. Race had a lot to do with it. We would tell collectors that he was an incredibly smart man. Their response was always, "Do you mean street-smart?" And we would say, "No, we mean smart." [156]

It seems like a totally arbitrary judgment, if I may be so bold, to look at a piece of art that is currently making waves with the masses and judge it as not worth considering. And I don't think much has changed in that world. The masses understand this intuitively: the art world pretends to judge things on some sort of objective scale, but nobody really knows anything about anything. It all really is in the eye of the beholder. Basquiat painted things that were inside him, period, and it worked—people liked it. The clunkiness of the museum establishment always seems to lag behind the natural momentum that the masses recognize instinctively, based on their immediate gut reactions to pieces of art, whether the piece is considered "proper" art or not. Basquiat's work appealed to both the masses and the intelligentsia, and the former made the latter uncomfortable, which of course was a clue that he was the real deal.

Madonna would say, of their time together, that Basquiat "loathed the idea that art was appreciated by an elite group. He used to say he was jealous of me because

---

[156]   *Jean-Michel Basquiat: The Radiant Child* (Davis, 2010)

music is more accessible and it reached more people." [157] Now this is the kind of artist I like—one that knows that the people are what matter. The masses matter; the ivory tower does not.

As his fame grew, his ability to exist in public spaces unbothered, shrank.

He moved to Los Angeles, gaining distance from his original neighborhood crew of Bohemian compatriots, some of whom were not exactly thrilled that he'd left. He would sometimes sell paintings before they were technically "finished" to meet the high demands of his backlist of buyers, and felt mounting pressure from within and without. He went from homeless to international star in the course of two or three years, and though exciting, it was also overwhelming.

In *The Radiant Child*, fellow artist and rival Julian Schnabel remarked, "In modern times, there is for sure, whether you take Jackson Pollock, whether you take Vincent Van Gogh, a romance about the notion of the artist as a person whose life is so intense that it's more than he can bear. And there is always the question of, *is it a kind of self-fulfilling prophecy?* And I think particularly in Basquiat's case, he identified very consciously with these heroes who had tragic endings." [158]

Here we see the insidious meme raise its ugly head, yet again, and worm its way into the brain of a pressured, early-20s prodigy, susceptible to ambition and with a desire to emulate his heroes. It is what many of

157   Ibid.
158   Ibid.

us would do, perhaps, if we were in his shoes, if we had his background and his desires. This narrative arc, of subjecting oneself to intense experience for inspiration, exists especially noticeably in the world of the arts.

"Inspiration" is the all-important aspect, and what better object to cling to than the chemicals and substances that your heroes promise is a shortcut to this inspiration? A friend from school, Martin Aubert, recalled a disturbingly foreshadowing talk he had with Basquiat that gives us a glimpse as to how infectious and tempting this narrative arc can be: "He was covered with paint and shivering. He said, I'm on heroin. I guess you don't approve of that, but I have decided the true path to creativity is to burn out. He mentioned Janis Joplin, Hendrix, Billie Holiday (1915–1959), Charlie Parker. I said, 'All those people are dead, Jean.' He said, 'If that's what it takes…' " [159] The ingredients were there for Basquiat—pressure, stress, a feeling of invincibility, infamy, and a culture that promoted drugs as the answer to all one's artistic ambitions. All that was needed for this to go over the edge was the right series of small pushes, which of course, arrived in due time.

The first was Michael Stewart (1958–1983), a young graffiti artist arrested for writing on the wall of a subway late at night. He was beaten into a coma by police, and later died in the hospital.

Stewart happened to have been a friend of Suzanne Mallouk, who had allowed Basquiat to live

159   "Burning Out," A. Haden-Guest, VanityFair.com, 2014.

with her nearly rent-free for many years in his early stages of development. Stewart was adjacent to the community in which Basquiat had cut his teeth, and Basquiat was deeply disturbed by the breaking of this news story. Stewart's lot in life was the exact position—a young graffiti artist hopping subways—that Basquiat himself had just been in only a few short years before. He realized that even at his extreme level of fame, if he walked out of his door and doodled on a wall the way he used to, and an officer did not recognize him, the same fate could easily befall him because of his race. Basquiat famously did a painting featuring the officers beating Stewart, immortalizing the dirty deed for generations to come.

"To go from a place where everyone knows who the hell you are and is looking at you, hoping to get laid by you, and to go back out in the world and to be just this black guy walking around looking kinda bummy to most people's eyes, that was a mindfuck." [160]

Basquiat began to notice, with this event and many others, that his skin color was a frustratingly omnipresent, limiting factor in both his life and career. He remarked: "Most of my reviews have been more reviews on my personality, more so than my work. They're just racist, most of these people—They have this image of me, you know, 'wild man,' 'wild monkey man,' whatever the fuck they say." [161] He was responding to numerous reviews and columns that would describe him

160   *Jean-Michel Basquiat: The Radiant Child* (Davis, 2010)
161   Ibid.

as "primitive" and a "wild boy," one interviewer going as far to call his residency in Annina Nosei's gallery as being "locked in the basement." "I've never been locked anywhere," [162] he said to this interviewer, becoming visibly (and understandably) uncomfortable.

One of his most iconic motifs is the three-pointed crown, found across his works and associated with kingly royalty, which he juxtaposed with black heritage and traditional black symbolism. In other words, a black king: something that was not a familiar symbol to American culture.

Meanwhile, amidst these disturbing realizations, he was still doing drugs. He found that his dream world of art fame was doing its best to exploit him for his monetary value, with or without his consent. "The parasites came," said Suzanne Mallouk, "Eventually, he became paranoid and started isolating himself—covering the windows of our apartment with black construction paper so that nobody could see in. He was worried that, as a famous African-American man, the CIA or the FBI would have him murdered. I expect that a lot of it had to do with the drugs." [163] In fame and in his exodus from the Downtown 500, he found himself without any "real" friends.

"I like to remain a little reclusive," he said, "and not just be out there, you know, just to be brought up and be brought down like they do to most of them. They

162   Ibid.
163   "American Graffiti," H. Maitland, Vogue.co.uk, 2017.

always [turn on you]. I can't think of one big celebrity type person that they haven't done that to." [164]

The one friend in this time that Basquiat felt he could rely on was Andy Warhol, partly because Warhol was completely enamored with him, but perhaps also because the problems Basquiat was having with authenticity and trust were familiar to someone on Warhol's level of fame. Warhol could relate to the strange problems that Basquiat was facing now that he was a worldwide fixture.

Eventually, they decided to properly collaborate, and this led to a large amount of pieces where they would paint and draw over each other in a sort of friendly/competitive visual banter.

This was cathartic for Basquiat because it seemed to be the answer to two kinds of isolation: the isolation of his drifting personal friendships, and the isolation of trying to penetrate a greater art world that was not always welcoming. There is a quote often attributed to Basquiat: "I am not a black artist. I am an artist." Although this quote has been widely shared, it is unclear exactly when, or even if, he said it. Nevertheless, it captures the essence of his message and says something about how we have chosen to remember him.

In a strange and spectacular fashion, however, his collaboration with his ultimate artistic hero (what was supposed to be the absolute, peak dream-come-true scenario) backfired. Andy had begun to drift out of vogue

164   *Jean-Michel Basquiat: The Radiant Child* (Davis, 2010)

in public opinion, and with him, Basquiat's collaboration was torn apart as over-hyped. The reviews were bad and the paintings did not sell.

To add tragedy to insult, Warhol passed away not long afterwards.

The storm was too perfect. Drugs, especially heroin, re-emerged with a vengeance as Basquiat's only escape. Around this time he became extremely isolated, and if lingering friends or his girlfriend would attempt to help him get clean, he would lash out at them.

"The pressure of that artificial world made it difficult for him to do something. 'They tell me the drugs are killing me, and then I stop, and then they say my art's dead.'" [165]

His last exhibition, two years later, contained a disturbing amount of death and dying imagery, and was sparse, melancholic, and bleak.

Near the end of his life, he would often go back to his father, still seeking to prove that he was successful. Though, in his later years, his relationship with his father deteriorated as well. There seemed to be some communication eternally lost between them.

He went back and tried to visit his old girlfriend Suzanne Mallouk and all his old friends back in Manhattan. He met with Diaz, presenting him with a painting that read, "to SAMO from SAMO." But his relationships had dissolved with time and distance; Diaz, much to his own personal shame, sold the painting

165   Ibid.

shortly after that interaction. In his words, "We started to drift apart, as you do with childhood friends. By 1979, he was hanging out more and more with what I thought of as the beautiful people."[166] He found himself worlds apart from his origins, and simultaneously alienated by his new world in Los Angeles.

In 1988, Basquiat collapsed in his NoHo studio. He died of a heroin overdose.

As of 2017, Basquiat holds the record for most expensive painting sale in any U.S. auction, for his "Untitled (1982)" which sold for 110,500,000.00 dollars[167] While I get a lot of flak for harping on about money all the time, let's let someone more credible in the art world say it, once and for all. In the words of Andy Warhol: "Being good in business is the most fascinating kind of art… Making money is art and working is art, and good business is the best art."[168] In the end, it seems, Basquiat's work triumphed over the ivory tower and the race lines the establishment attempted to draw. The crowns on his paintings might as well be made of real gold now for how they are valued. Those who knew him believe he would be pleased with this result. He had more to say, always more to say, and it is a shame that he doesn't get to say any more.

166   "American Graffiti," Maitland, Vogue.co.uk, 2017.
167   "A Basquiat Sells for 'Mind-Blowing' $110.5 Million at Auction," by Robin Pogrebin and Scott Reyburn, *New York Times*, 05/18/2017.
168   "The Business Artist: How Andy Warhol Turned a Love of Money Into a $228 Million Art Career," by ARTINFO, HuffingtonPost.com, 12/16/2010.

Kurt Cobain

1967 – 1994

"Holding my baby is the best drug in the world. We have a lot of young fans and I don't want to have anything to do with inciting drug use. People who promote drug use are assholes. I chose to do drugs. I don't feel sorry for myself at all, but have nothing good to say about them. They are a total waste of time."

-KURT COBAIN[169]

169   "Kurt Cobain (1992): Cobain to Fans: Just Say No," by Robert Hilburn, LATimes.com, 09/11/1992.

Kurt Cobain

Kurt Cobain is arguably the most oft-referenced name when the subject of the 27 club comes up, a figure that fans hold up as emblematic of romanticized tragedy and the "tortured artist." He is often credited with that famous quotable of all quotables, "It is better to burn out than fade away," from his suicide note (though this quote was actually a Neil Young lyric).[170] Cobain's death made almost as many waves as his music, because his rise and fall seemed to correspond with the genesis and demise of grunge's moment in history, and of a particular generation's point of view. Whereas other subgenres of rock can be debated, grunge has a single undisputed figurehead, and that is Cobain.

---

170   "Neil Young: 'Being Mentioned in Kurt Cobain's Suicide Note Fucked With Me,'" by *NME* editors, NME.com, 09/11/2012.

In 1993, we were putting together an album of artists that wanted to cover KISS songs, just for the fun of it. Garth Brooks (b.1962), Lenny Kravitz (b.1964), Stevie Wonder (b.1950), and quite a few others joined in. Of course, by the time the various record companies that had exclusive rights to these artists got wind of it, there were restrictions thrown at us. But we got by.

I had heard a bootleg, a fan-made KISS tribute album, and among one of the covers was none other than Nirvana doing a wonderfully trashy, punk take on our song, "Do You Love Me." And I thought it was great. Even being tongue-in-cheek, even as it poked fun at us—the old school macho rockers that were at the time the natural enemy of the grunge movement, which I can appreciate—it was undeniably great.

The 90s were a period of transition. Bands that had been around a long time were swept away by bands that were playing punk-inspired rock without the fancy production. Nirvana made the biggest impact in that regard. There is no denying that their songwriting and musical talent was top notch.

So I decided to try to track the boys down and ask them to be on our cover album. I never use managers or agents to look people up or make my phone calls for me—I just dive into the deep end of the pool. Sometimes it works, sometimes not, but the interactions are always interesting.

One thing to note here is Nirvana's, and particularly Cobain's, penchant for practical jokes. His close friend Buzz Osbourne called Cobain, "A master at jerking your chain." [171] So keep that in mind.

I recall that the phone line wasn't all that clear on the day I called Kurt Cobain, but I got through. Cobain and I were talking, and I have to admit I was surprised and flattered by how nice he seemed. That's what they say about some of these "legendary anti-heroes"; people who meet them are often caught off guard that they are *people* at all, people with compassion and personalities with as much nuance as our own. Speaking to someone is the most humanizing act of all, I suppose. I started discussing which song they may want to record, and so on. The good-natured phone call ended with, "Let's reconvene and we'll figure it out." I wished them well and hung up the phone.

But sadly, Kurt Cobain had passed before we ever got a chance to interact again, and Nirvana did not appear on the album I was putting together. There was a lot going on with both of us. This phone call would be our only extended interaction.

Yet, years later, I started reading articles and interviews by the remaining band members of Nirvana, including Pat Thrall who played guitar with Nirvana and continued to play with Dave Grohl (b.1969) and the Foo Fighters. And I found it peculiar that Thrall mentioned that he recalled my telephone call, but said *he* was pretending to be Cobain, with the rest of the band laughing audibly in the background. He said he was pulling my leg the whole time. Cue the *wah-wah-wah*.

171   "Buzz Osborne (the Melvins) Talks the HBO Documentary 'Kurt Cobain: Montage of Heck,'" by Buzz Osborne, Talkhouse.com, 06/06/2015.

To this day, I have no idea if it was actually Cobain, or if it was Thrall pranking me. Maybe Mr. Grohl can set it all straight some day. But I include this story to show the other side of these guys, a side that gets shoved under the rug, especially when it comes to Cobain: they were funny. They liked being sardonic, sarcastic, poking holes and fun at establishment and celebrity and everything people consider important. You can see this attitude in any television interview with the band (all of which Cobain seemed to despise and mock). The man refused to let anyone throw their weight around in front of him, and refused to let anyone else take themselves too seriously. I find this a charming part of their legacy (even if it was at my expense), true to their punk roots, and I think it's a shame that this lighthearted part takes a back seat to the tragedy of his end. I think it's important to understand this punk prankster aspect to understand the man.

The story of Nirvana's rise and Kurt's descent has been oft-repeated, and there are better and more detailed biographies out there than I could ever write. But a summary is necessary, and I decided to go primarily to the only documentary authorized by the Cobain family, Brett Morgen's *Montage of Heck*, to get these details, as opposed to reading the various conspiratorial biopics and exposés, which never seem to run out of steam. The stated goal of this documentary was to drain the mythology away, to show the man as a man. This is my goal too. Almost everyone, when reflecting on figures like

Cobain, seem to project certain heroic narratives onto them. Cobain was a human being, and it may not have ever crossed his mind or been desirable to him to be a hero. As Spencer Kornhaber writes in *The Atlantic*:

> Assuming causes and effects that can't ever be known, turning a human being into an abstraction: *Montage of Heck* [...] was created specifically to ward against this sort of thing. In 2007, Courtney Love gave [Brett] Morgen access to a trove of previously unexamined recordings, notes, and artwork relating to her late husband, with one bit of instruction that would take the director eight years to carry out. [Love said] "It was time to examine this person and humanize him and decanonize these values that he allegedly stood for—the lack of ambition and these ridiculous myths that had been built up around him." [172]

Cobain grew up in Aberdeen, Washington, a town known for high suicide rates and alcoholism, foreshadowing the dark moods of Cobain and the musical movement that was to come. However, the infant Kurt was reportedly an extremely bright, cheerful, hyper-energetic, and magnetic child. His defining characteristic from a young age was simply compassion; he worried about people and their well-being.

172   "Embracing the Myth of Kurt Cobain," by Spencer Kornhaber, TheAtlantic.com, 04/24/2015.

For a time, things were good—Norman-Rockwell-nuclear-family good—until they were not. As Morgen put it:

> Wendy described problems starting around 2 1/2, 3, with his hyperactivity. And it was an age where I think all boys are hyperactive, you know? He had very young parents, I think 18, 20 years old; they were still babies themselves for all practical purposes. Kurt started to have problems with hyperactivity that happened right around the time his sister was born, and so they took him to a doctor, and the doctor initially prescribed Ritalin, and when that didn't prove effective, they tried sedatives, and when that didn't prove effective, they tried removing him from sugar, and depending on who you're talking to, there are a lot of different attempts made to regulate Kurt's energy if you will. Coupled with that, Wendy [his mother] talks about in the film that Don [his father], in particular, had a real hard time handling Kurt and his hyperactivity, and would sort of ridicule him, occasionally hit him around the head, or smack him around a little bit.[173]

When his parents divorced, when Kurt was aged nine, he was "embarrassed to death,"[174] and began acting

---

173   "Kurt Cobain Speaks, Through Art and Audio Diaries, In 'Montage of Heck,'" by *NPR* staff, NPR.org, 05/03/2015.
174   *Montage of Heck* (US, 2015), dir. Brett Morgen, prod. HBO Documentary Films, 145 min.

out more than usual. He was eventually sent to live with his father and step-family, but this did nothing to comfort Kurt's desire for a unified home. He was sent to live with other family members, but nothing seemed to quell his frustration that his parents' marriage had dissolved. His sister, Kim, summed up his dilemma well: "He wanted normalcy; he wanted the mom, the dad, and the kids and everything happy. But then, he didn't. He kind of fought against it. He fought against what he really wanted." [175] As a kind of defense mechanism, it seemed, he met rejection with a stronger rejection. If he was to be denied the secure, traditional family he had had in infancy, then he would rebel against it; that seemed to be his only defense against the humiliation of it all. In a recorded conversation with Buzz Osborne, Cobain reminisced about their shared hellish high school experience: "I quit the last two months of school. I was so withdrawn by that time and I was so antisocial that I was almost insane. You know, I felt so different and so crazy that people just left me alone." [176]

He self-medicated the growing anxiety and panic he felt with marijuana, but found that this was a Band-Aid, not a cure. "I accumulated quite a healthy complex. I could escape all day long [by smoking pot] and not have routine nervous breakdowns. During that month happened to be the epitome of my mental abuse from my mother. It turned out that pot didn't help me escape my troubles too well anymore and I was actually enjoying doing rebellious things like stealing booze and busting

175   *Montage of Heck* (Morgen, 2015)
176   Ibid.

store windows. And nothing ever mattered."[177] It was around this time that Cobain began talking about killing himself—whether in jest, as close friend Buzz Osborne later insisted, or in seriousness, it is hard to say.

Cobain often claimed to experience an undiagnosed stomach illness that caused him extreme pain throughout his life. Some have said that this is why he turned to heroin, as a way to numb the pain, though others, like Osborne, say it is the other way around: "He made it up for sympathy and so he could use it as an excuse to stay loaded. Of course he was vomiting—that's what people on heroin do, they vomit."[178] According to *Montage of Heck*, Kurt attempted suicide in his early teens after being bullied, laying down on railroad tracks only to have the train take an adjacent track and spare him. However, Osborne says that this, too, was simply Cobain being "a master at jerking your chain."[179]

"Every time I've had an endoscope, they'd find a red irritation. I would sing and cough up blood. It's like, this is no way to live a life... So, I decided to medicate myself."[180] A journal entry says, "For five years every single day an ongoing stomach ailment had literally taken me to the point of wanting to kill myself."[181]

Cobain lived in varying levels of poverty and squalor after high school. However, he would not be

177   Ibid.
178   "Buzz Osborne (the Melvins)," Osborne, Talkhouse.com, 2015.
179   "'90 Percent of 'Montage of Heck' is Bulls-t,' Says Melvin Founder,'" by Miriam Coleman, RollingStone.com, 06/06/2015.
180   *Montage of Heck* (Morgen, 2015)
181   Ibid.

alone for long; there was a growing community of like-minded young people who felt dissatisfied with their lives in the same way he did, and this mood would congeal into a new sort of counterculture—one based not on free love, like the hippies, but on dissatisfaction and a rejection of the status quo put in place by the previous generation. Cobain discovered punk rock: "It expressed the way I felt socially and politically, and it was the anger that I felt, the alienation." [182]

The band formed, first as a garage band, jamming for hours for a rotating cast of friends who would wander in. Despite Cobain's seemingly erroneous reputation as a slacker who simply wanted to rebel and goof off, bandmate Krist Novoselic (b.1965) speaks of a different man: a true creative who could not help but make things, draw things, paint things, and record things in whatever medium was available. "He was working at the time as a janitor. He'd always have to do some kind of art, usually defacing something. He never had idle hands. It just came out of him; he had to express himself." [183]

Nirvana eventually went on tour, existing on pennies, and released their first album with enough moderate success to justify more steady touring. Even in the early days, Cobain had a preoccupation with public humiliation, and so was guarded about how he and the band were presented. Gradually, they garnered critical buzz, and attracted the attention of labels and industry.

"I think it's embarrassing to have so many

---

182   Ibid.
183   Ibid.

expectations," Cobain said at the time, "and it's a totally superficial label to put on a band to state that they're 'the next big thing,' because that's not our goal in the first place. People are putting that tag on us without us really wanting to do that, you know? We're prepared to destroy our careers if it happens." [184]

This buzzy time was around when Grohl joined the group. It was not until the next album, the more pop-friendly *Nevermind* and its single, "Smells Like Teen Spirit," that the group became a household name.

Grohl recalled what touring immediately after the release of *Nevermind* was like in a 2014 interview with him and Novoselic on the *The Tonight Show:*

> We were booked into these places and some of them held, like, 90 people, some of them were 150 people, and we'd pull up in our van, and because our album had come out and the video was on MTV and stuff, we'd pull up and there'd be so many people trying to get into the show that even when we had a gold record, we were still in a van with a U-Haul trailer. So it happened really quickly and it was really weird.[185]

It must have been hard to adjust. "The runaway success was like suddenly discovering that the car was a Ferrari and the accelerator pedal was Krazy Glued to the floorboard. Friends worried about how the band

---

184   Ibid.
185   Dave Grohl, *The Tonight Show Starring Jimmy Fallon*, 04/14/2014.

was dealing with it all," [186] according to a *Rolling Stone* magazine interview with Cobain in 1992. While Cobain insisted he was taking it fine, he had a problem with the sudden mantle he had acquired as the megaphone of his generation's angst. Nils Bernstein, a friend who helped them sort fan mail, remarked, "People are treating him like a god, and that pisses him off... They're giving Kurt this elevated sense of importance that he feels he doesn't have or deserve." [187] When asked about being a spokesman for a generation of young people, Cobain dismissed it: "I'm a spokesman for myself. It just so happens that there's a bunch of people that are concerned with what I have to say. I find that frightening at times because I'm just as confused as most people. I don't have the answers for anything. I don't want to be a fucking spokesperson." [188]

This mentality—this rejection of traditional markers of success—never made sense to me as a younger man; I think that goes without saying. I never understood the luxury of being able to worry about an abstract concept like a punk ethos; I was just glad anyone wanted to pay me to play, and I've always loved talking my head off to anyone who would listen. Different strokes, as they say. I came from a different generation, a different type of community; I was an immigrant obsessed with the unironic America I saw on television, and I was ready

186   "Nirvana: Inside the Heart and Mind of Kurt Cobain," by Michael Azerrad, *Rolling Stone*, 04/16/1992.
187   *Montage of Heck* (Morgen, 2015)
188   "Nirvana: Inside the Heart," Azerrad, *Rolling Stone*, 1992.

and willing to gobble up the Dream whole. Perhaps this was the same America that Cobain found so unpleasant. Suburban angst, internal, introspective pain, the pain of artistic integrity never resonated with me—I came from a home with bullet holes in it, and escaping that seemed all-consuming, the rest unimportant. All problems are relative, but there are ways of putting mental health and problems of "art" and "self-actualization" on the back-burner when one has more physical, base dangers to worry about. Myself and some of my ilk were comfortable with materialism, with wealth, with a proud capitalist ideal, with being "rock stars." It suited us. But Cobain was never comfortable with this power, this lottery that he hit, though he had the looks, the songwriting and musicianship chops, and the success. I was never in a position to understand where he was coming from. In essence, my childhood feelings were slightly too low on the hierarchy of needs to even consider the sorts of things that Cobain found so painful. So, at the time, me and a few of my contemporaries from the 70s and 80s judged the grunge mantras rather harshly, though we did actually like the songs. Those of us from previous decades were positioned as the natural enemy of this new sound, which dressed down in an anti-theatricality, anti-showmanship chic, and who sang about anger and pain as opposed to sex and grandstanding. Cobain disliked the macho and ultra-hetero mentalities from music's earlier years and from the people around him in Aberdeen, before he was ever in a band. He resented the bullying and pressures he felt to be a certain sort of person in his teens, so it was no surprise that music that espoused these values did not speak to him. "In a community that stresses macho, male sexual stories as a highlight of all conversation, I was an underdeveloped, immature little dude that never got laid and was constantly razzed." [189]

Singing about inherently depressing things just didn't hit my generation. But it spoke to people of his time, and they bought those records because they felt connected to what Cobain had to say and his songwriting, even if he did not necessarily want to be their leader. In the end, that's all that really matters. No matter what message you do or do not identify with, Cobain was talented. However, this friction—between his ethos, his discomfort with corporate materialism, and his commercial success—tortured him, because, like it or not, he was both hugely successful and influential. It would continue to torture him throughout his life. Finding happiness at the top, it seems, was not an option for someone who was so disgusted with the traditional markers of a good life (female attention, fans, money), even when that happiness was there for the taking.

Novoselic seemed to sum it up best. "I guess each individual's going to deal with it the way they're going to deal with it. It was kind of traumatic being famous all of a sudden. I did things like withdraw or drink. You know, I'm lucky, I had beer and wine, you know? Kurt had heroin." [190]

The fact that I am not in a position to understand where Cobain's angst came from regarding a situation

---

189   *Montage of Heck* (Morgen, 2015)
190   Ibid.

that I feel wonderful about is precisely the point. We are different people, with different life experiences and different values—life is full of menus, and not all of us want to order the same thing. Fame and commercial success, it seemed, were dishes Cobain never expected to have to swallow, things he never requested.

At some point in 1992, Cobain married a pregnant Courtney Love in a small ceremony in Hawaii. Novoselic explains why it all happened so fast: "I had this relationship, with this woman [and] I just kind of wanted to build this home for myself, because my home growing up had fallen apart. I think that Kurt wanted to do that too. He wanted to build a home, because his home and his family fell apart." [191] The couple reportedly began using heroin again, though Kurt denied it in a 1992 *Rolling Stone* interview.

"He wanted to stay in the apartment and do heroin and paint. And play his guitar. That's what he wanted to do," said Love later, "[and] we were all we had, so making a family as fast as possible was, you know, important." [192]

Unfortunately, Cobain's heroin use began to bleed into his professional life, and the lives of his bandmates. Among other anecdotes, he once fell asleep during a photo shoot for *Saturday Night Live* before the band was scheduled to perform. [193]

The tabloids were rampant with rumors that

191   Ibid.
192   Ibid.
193   *Come As You Are: The Story of Nirvana*, by Michael Azerrad (Doubleday, US: 1993)

the couple was using while Love was pregnant. Cobain and Love would make home videos, and write letters, slamming the press for being "vicious" and "parasites." [194] Needless to say, the attention and the shaming did nothing to help Cobain's self-medication. When asked how it felt to have his "inevitable self-destruction" rubbed in their face every day in the media, Cobain recalled the childhood angst that had shaped his personality (and his drug habit) to begin with. "It makes you feel like the kid in school who gets picked on all the time, or it makes you feel like the school slut." [195]

Child services, in response to a *Vanity Fair* article that claimed Love was using heroin while pregnant, attempted to seize the newborn child, but Cobain and Love soon regained custody. The birth was life-changing for Cobain, who wrote that he would, "Fight to the death to keep the right to provide for my child. I'll go out of my way to remind her that I love her more than I love myself. Not because it's a father's duty but because I want to—out of love."[196]

Cobain was, by this time, only happy in the home he had built for himself with Love and their new baby. The outside world was a mess of paranoia, and of music journalists trying to get the dirtiest and most shameful scoop they could. The battle for their child was always ongoing, with the couple having to submit to regular urine tests to retain custody.

---

194   *Montage of Heck* (Morgen, 2015)
195   *Montage of Heck* (Morgen, 2015)
196   Ibid.

By the release of *In Utero* (which opens with "Serve the Servants," a song that includes lyrics skewering the tabloid coverage as a witch hunt), Cobain's depressive and paranoid spiral had reached a fever pitch of illusion, negative feelings, and self-medication. He started going back home to his mother's, in her words, "to hide," covered in sores and nodding off; his mother described him, yet again, as being "ashamed," [197] the emotion he was so intimately familiar with from his upbringing.

With no experience in addiction myself, I cannot empathize with this situation. I can only remark that it must have been very strange for someone so affected by the words of the outside world (words that I luckily have been able to ignore my entire life) to have an album release that soars and is critically-acclaimed, while simultaneously the same critics relish tales of your downward spiral. It seems to be a rather mixed message, and for someone so affected by feedback, it was probably intolerable.

The band did a live concert recording for MTV's *Unplugged*, a concert that to this day has been hailed as one of the greatest of its kind, because of its vulnerability and Cobain's wailing, pained vocal—somehow better for being strained, shaking, and audibly raw. The highlight of this session is widely considered to be Nirvana's rendition of "Where Did You Sleep Last Night," an old Negro spiritual song that was popularized by Lead Belly, who Cobain describes in the recording as "my favorite

197   Ibid.

performer." [198] Once again, the influence of blues cannot be overstated. The lyrics are about murder, but I cannot help but think of romantic jealousy when I hear Cobain sing it; Love says in *Montage of Heck* that she once broke Cobain's heart by only thinking of cheating on him.[199]

Cobain is visibly nervous in the footage, which only made the fans love him more. "We're all sensitive to ridicule and shame," says Morgen in *Montage of Heck,* "but it seemed to me, having gone through his materials, that he was hypersensitive; felt criticism, felt praise, felt things a little more intensely." Courtney Love concurred.

Love once called the police to their home in Seattle because Cobain had locked himself in a closet with a gun. For this incident, Love later blamed herself: "When he came home from Rome high, I flipped out. If there's one thing in my whole life I could take back, it would be that. Getting mad at him for coming home high. I wish to God I hadn't. I wish I'd just been the way I always was, just tolerant of it. It made him feel so worthless when I got mad at him." [200]

Courtney would later arrange a tense intervention that would end with Cobain submitting himself into Exodus Recovery Center in LA. After a day, he hopped the fence and flew himself back to Seattle. Love and his friends searched for him to no avail.

On the morning of April 8th, Cobain's body was

---

198   Kurt Cobain, Nirvana—*MTV Unplugged*, 11/18/1992.
199   *Montage of Heck* (Morgen, 2015)
200   "Courtney Love: Life Without Kurt," by David Fricke, RollingStone.com, 12/15/1994.

found by an electrician at his home in Seattle. He had taken his own life with a shotgun. In his blood were high doses of heroin and Valium.[201]

In our mythologizing of him and the "tortured artist" character, I think we forget to ask a deceptively obvious question, a question that people simply seem to take as axiomatic. Yes, it is true that Cobain made great rock music, and suffered. But the question is, did he make great music *because* he suffered? Do any of the personal issues illustrated above *necessitate* good music? Or art? Or legendary status? It's a question Cobain was asked during an interview. His response was telling: "See, that's a scary question, because I think it probably helps, you know? But I would give up everything to have good health. But then again, I'm always afraid that if I lost the stomach problem I might not be as creative."[202] It seemed he didn't know the true answer, but also did not necessarily like the implication that his suffering (in that interview they spoke about his stomach pain specifically) was a necessary evil for making art. As he said: it's a scary question.

I believe one could find oneself having all the same personal issues, all the same strifes, doing all the same drugs, and still making a subpar piece of music—a record that hits no one in the soul or speaks to no one's experience. So many of our heroes follow

201   "Kurt Cobain's Downward Spiral: The Last Days of Nirvana's Leader," by Neil Strauss, RollingStone.com, 06/02/1994.
202   *Montage of Heck* (Morgen, 2015)

such similar paths and have such hard lives that it is easy to associate the pain and the illness with the genius, but this is correlation, not causation. Sure, having something to write about does "help." But Cobain does not give himself enough credit, in my opinion, with his quote. He had a musical point of view, a style of songwriting, a personality, and a vibe, with or without his heroin addiction or his stomach pain. We can credit that to Cobain: Cobain the man, not an outside force or an affliction.

The high death rate in the young famous musician pool seems to come as much from the fame aspect as it does from the mental strife, because fame adds pressure to vulnerable individuals and proceeds to fuel (and fund) the continuation of a lifestyle that would be unsustainable in any other income bracket. The fact is that drug addiction and depression and angst are everywhere. They are a common feature of life itself, and it is only when such a person also happens to have a stroke of creativity, which then resonates with the masses, that we suddenly pay lots of attention to their drug use, as though we are all looking for a magic pill that will turn us into Kurt Cobain. But there is no such pill, because what he was happened before the pills and before the syringes. What made those songs so good was not the substances in his blood; it *was* his blood. The songs were made because he was the individual he was, with the thoughts only he could think and the music only he could make. I think looking at it this way is much more *romantic* than looking at it the way people tend to: as suicide and self-inflicted pain being necessary, causally-related symptoms of tortured genius. That is not how Cobain's loved ones, the ones close enough to actually feel the effects, would want to look at it, and it is not how the man himself looked at it either. Later in life, when Cobain was in the midst of tabloid hysteria, he remarked, "I feel like people want me to die because it would be the classic rock and roll story."[203] Clearly, he felt the pressure of the narrative that seems to come out of the ether and pressure people to conform to it. Grohl would remark that there was nothing mythical or magical to him about the death of his friend and bandmate: "[It was] probably the worst thing that has happened to me in my life. I just felt like, 'Okay, so I get to wake up today and have another day and he doesn't.'"[204]

In 2015, *The Telegraph* ran an article titled "Kurt Cobain was not a 'tortured genius,' he had an illness." In it, the author himself admitted that in his "immaturity, I thought there was something cool about it."[205] He remarks that the "myth has probably sold a lot of records over the years [...] creative talent and tormented minds, we are told, are sides of the same coin."[206] The author goes on to illustrate what influenced his change of heart—the fact that he fell into depression and attempted suicide at 24 years of age. He found his own, first-hand

203   "Embracing the Myth of Kurt Cobain," Kornhaber, TheAtlantic.com, 2015.
204   "Dave Grohl: 'I Knew Kurt Cobain Was Destined to Die Early,'"NME. co.uk, 11/10/2009.
205   "Kurt Cobain Was Not a 'Tortured Genius', He Had An Illness," by Matt Haig, Telegraph.co.uk, 04/05/2018.
206   Ibid.

experience of pain to be decidedly unglamorous. In, fact, he found his own mental illness "exactly as glamorous as physical illness." [207]

> Not long before Cobain shot himself he had been hospitalised due to bronchitis [...] Bronchitis, in almost all our minds, remains as unglamorous as ever, no matter how many rock stars suffer from it. I would love it if death-by-depression was seen in exactly the same way as death-by-bronchitis. It should be. Because glamorising suicide is almost as unhealthy as demonising it. It inhibits our understanding.[208]

One of the cures for this, according to the author, is simply conversation. Demystifying something that should be no more or less sexy than a stomach condition is a big step toward having the right public attitude toward these ailments, and will weed out those who pretend to be depressed as a fashion statement, who undermine people who actually struggle with depression and want out. Cobain struggled with depression, bronchitis, stomach problems, and self-medicated with drugs, developing a serious drug addiction. These factors ushered him toward a young death. Yes, this is all less romantic than a punk rocker's last stand against corporate machinery, but it is also more likely to be the truth, and it is a truth that is important for us all to learn. To stop glamorizing

207   Ibid.
208   Ibid.

the 27 club, and to stop spreading the myth and the worship of young death, we must know that these are the unromantic, unsexy things that cause these young deaths. If we worship, let us worship the lives, not the deaths.

Incidentally, it seems Cobain himself would agree. He wanted nothing to do with a seductive club of death. Though he struggled with demons, he did not try to glamorize them. "I never went out of my way to say anything about my drug use," he said. "I think people who glamorize drugs are fucking assholes, and if there's a hell, they'll go there." People glamorized his drug use for him anyway, against his wishes. Kim Cobain recalled that, "Kurt's biggest fear was that he would inspire or influence kids to do heroin." [209] This was why Morgen included a few very disturbing-looking home videos of Cobain, with sores, nodding off. He said:

> Without that image, we're once again just propagating this myth, because everyone knows Kurt's associated with heroin, but we haven't seen the face of it. The idea was not to tear him down, nor was it to put him on a pedestal. It was just simply to look him in the eye, and I feel that when you strip away the layers of mythology and reveal the man, the man is so much more endearing and dynamic than the myth. One of the things the film shows is that Kurt's problems predated Courtney and they

209   "Kurt Cobain Speaks," *NPR* staff, NPR.org, 2015.

predated Frances and they predated fame and heroin and Nirvana.[210]

I think it is time we honor what he said he wanted, for once; let's stop putting the drugs and the depression on a pedestal, and equating them with the human being behind them. This is a lesson that I, specifically, have had to learn, but better late than never. I applaud Cobain for his concern about influencing kids, and I regret my previous misunderstanding of the man. His quote has certainly earned my respect. Just because someone has a deep well of personal problems, and makes mistakes, it does not necessarily mean they are a bad influence or a bad person. It just means they are a person.

210   Ibid.

Amy Winehouse

1983 – 2011

"You're just feeling it…
You don't think about it.
If you thought about it,
you wouldn't be able
to sing at all."

-AMY WINEHOUSE[211]

211   "Amy Winehouse: The Final Interview," by Neil McCormick, Telegraph.co.uk, 07/23/2011.

Amy
Winehouse

Winehouse is, to some old purists, a controversial addition to this list. To many, the 27 club is associated not only with musicians who died at the peak of their career, but also with a particular era in pop culture history: the late 60s to the 90s. As the years have passed, Winehouse's inclusion in this list has become more normalized.

For my part, I think this misses the point. The mistake in even having that conversation is that we still treat the 27 club list as its name suggests: as a *club*. Debating whether she belongs among the others implies an insidious notion—that the club is something one would *want* to get into. So, I won't bother arguing a point that includes an implication that I find morally repugnant.

The real point is, this is a talented young woman who died in her 20s. Her passing was not a medal, a Grammy, it was not a Rock & Roll Hall of Fame induction, or a star on the Hollywood Walk of Fame. She was a person, and she made music, and she died young.

I remember first seeing and hearing Amy Winehouse in a music video on VH1. Music videos had long ceased to be the events they once were. They were background noise as we all went on with our lives. I've made a fuss about this in the press, and it is no secret that there is a type of mainstream pop (or as I like to call it, disco-by-any-other-name) that makes me roll my eyes. For a long time, that was the top of the food chain.

But hold on there, I thought, one night as the background noise played. What's that sound? I remember thinking, "That voice. There's no way that's a contemporary artist."

I looked up and to my surprise I found a brand new singer, with a fully developed stage persona. That juxtaposition, of wounded bird covered in tattoos, dressed up to look badass—it floored me. What a great look, and the name! I had no idea it was actually her birth name. It struck me the way Johnny Rotten's name did—a genius bit of marketing that made a statement. It seemed she emerged from birth fully formed, like Hendrix: no stylist needed, no stage name. She was clearly born for this.

There were plenty of sugary pop princesses singing broken-heart lyrics and dancing alongside choreographed disco boys; this Winehouse character was having none of that. And I was hooked.

There was a clear, heart-on-her-sleeve DNA

lineage to the greats of yesteryear—people like Dinah Washington and Billie Holiday. And when I heard Winehouse do a duet with Tony Bennett (b.1926), the man Sinatra called the best singer in the world, it became clear that this (then) 26-year-old could hold her own next to one of the giants of music. Like many on this list: if you saw her sing, it was undeniable.

Winehouse was born in London and raised on an eclectic mix of R&B, jazz, and blues. She loved Thelonius Monk (1917–1982), Carole King (b.1942), and Tony Bennett, and felt an almost total disconnect from the pop music of her youth. "The music that was in the pop charts, I just thought, 'This isn't music. This is watered down. Just crap. Someone else has written it for you and you have to sing it,'" she said. "It's very much the case with some music today. I felt like I had nothing new that was coming out at the time that really represented me or the way I felt."[212] I have to say, I empathize with that. Her decision to write her own music was, in her own words, a challenge to herself to see if she had anything new to say that had not already been said by the jazz greats of old.

Her influences, it seemed, did not come out of nowhere. Many members of her extended family were seasoned jazz musicians, so she was immersed from a young age in music from before her time, which would influence her foray into a new kind of pop-soul singing.[213]

---

212   *Amy* (UK, 2016), dir. Asif Kapadia, prod. Film4, 128 min.
213   "Amy Winehouse," Biography.com, accessed: 06/01/2018.

She was an easygoing child until her parents separated, in the midst of an almost decade-long affair her father had engaged in. After, by her estimation, the age of nine, there was a noticeable change in her personality. She began dressing differently and being more rebellious. She was taken to her doctor and eventually prescribed antidepressants. In her words, "I don't think I knew what depression was. I knew I felt funny sometimes and I was different. I think it's a musician thing. That's why I write music. There is [sic] a lot of people that suffer depression that don't have an outlet—that can't pick up a guitar for an hour and feel better." [214]

She attended a prestigious performing arts school, the Sylvia Young Theatre School in London, but was expelled for piercing her nose, among other things.[215]

Before her career took off, she did not consider singing to be a way to make her living. She thought of it more as a personal pleasure, something she could always do, and always have, much more like therapy or medicine than a viable income stream.[216] "I write songs because I'm fucked up in the head and I need to put it on paper and then write a song to it and to feel better about it— have something good out of something bad." [217]

Winehouse was known to self-deprecate, calling herself "ugly" in numerous interviews.[218] In two of the

214   *Amy* (Kapadia, 2016)
215   "Amy Winehouse Bio," Rolling Stone editors, RollingStone.com, accessed: 06/01/2018.
216   *Amy* (Kapadia, 2016)
217   Ibid.
218   "A Bad Girl With a Touch of Genius," by Guy Trebay, *New York Times*, 07/27/2011.

very first clips in the Oscar-winning documentary *Amy*, the singer is shown playing around with a camcorder, along with friend and manager Nick Shymansky, in a recording studio. It never takes her very long, it seems, before she sees herself in the screen and remarks, "I look ugly, Nicky," while trying to fix her hair.[219] In another clip, she films herself smoking, laughing, joking, and singing—throwing in, "I look so grim." [220]

Her break came from a chance created by a friend who happened to forward a demo tape she had recorded onto an A&R man. When she landed her first publishing deal, she was most excited about finally having her own apartment, away from her mother's house, in which she could "smoke weed all day" and write songs.[221]

When asked how "big" she thought she was going to be, she was self-deprecating as ever: "I don't, at all. My music is not on that scale. Sometimes I wish it was but I don't think I'm going to be at all famous. I don't think I could handle it. I'd probably go mad." [222]

Although she seemed at times shy and insecure with her physical appearance, she took little guff from anyone who tried to put her in a box. If she ever felt she was being spoken down to or misrepresented, she would puff out her chest and proclaim her identity, which was a fully-developed persona from the very first record. "I've

219   *Amy* (Kapadia, 2016)
220   Ibid.
221   Ibid.
222   Ibid.

got my own style, and I write my own songs. You know, if someone has so much of something already, there's very little you can add." [223]

Her reputation as a real, raw, old soul with a golden voice attracted the attention of the media, and soon, the public. Hip hop artist Mos Def, a.k.a. Yasiin Bey (b.1973), heard the stories and came to see her, and the two became fast friends.

It was in Camden, in the new apartment she was so proud of, surrounded by the trendy music scene featuring the likes of the Kills and the Libertines, where she met Blake Fielder-Civil, her on-again-off-again boyfriend and future husband. The two became physically inseparable. "I liked to sabotage myself and Amy liked to sabotage herself. Maybe that was our nature," Fielder-Civil said, of the first summer they spent together. "She said her dad leaving her mum was what caused this. I said I understood. I cut my wrists when I was nine years old. I don't know if I wanted to necessarily die, I just wanted my mum to leave my stepdad. Me and Amy were quite similar." [224]

This would be the beginning of a war zone of a relationship. They would "repeatedly break each other's hearts," [225] and when it would get bad, Winehouse would reportedly be inconsolable, and turn to excessive drinking to numb her heartache. Fielder-Civil would become the subject of many of the more well-known songs Winehouse would go on to write.

223   Ibid.
224   Ibid.
225   Ibid.

Their first major falling out, when Fielder-Civil decided not to leave his then-girlfriend for Winehouse, would result in the first time Winehouse was presented with the option of rehab. She initially agreed, under the condition that her father approved. However, when her father was asked, he said to her manager, "She doesn't need to go to rehab, she's fine." In Amy's words, "My dad did actually go, 'You're all right, don't need to go.' So I said, 'All right, Dad, I'll go and meet him, and then we'll back out.' " [226] A line referencing this episode would later appear in her infamous song, "Rehab," "if my daddy thinks I'm fine."

After the documentary *Amy* premiered, in which the above quote appears, Winehouse's father Mitch was not happy with his portrayal, claiming selective editing portrayed him as a heartless enabler. The family has followed suit and, after initially giving the documentary their full blessing, has disavowed it. "They are trying to portray me in the worst possible light," Mitch Winehouse said to *The Guardian*. "It was 2005. Amy had fallen—she was drunk and banged her head. She came to my house, and her manager came round and said: 'She's got to go to rehab.' But she wasn't drinking every day. She was like a lot of kids, going out binge-drinking. And I said: 'She doesn't need to go to rehab.' In the film, I'm relating the story, and what I said was: 'She didn't need to go to

---

226   Ibid.

rehab *at that time.*' " [227]

Shymansky had a different take on the interaction, as seen in the documentary in which the above anecdote appears:

> I think that was the moment we lost a very key opportunity. I'm not saying it would've worked. Very often, you have to go two or three times. But she wasn't a star, she wasn't swarmed by paparazzi. We could have just fucked [the upcoming album] *Back to Black* off and *Back to Black* might have never happened, but she'd have had a chance to have been dealt with by professionals before the world wanted a piece of her.[228]

The album, *Back to Black,* by all accounts came from the dark, vulnerable moments after Amy's first big break from Fielder-Civil. As she was swarmed with negative feelings, her creativity blossomed; according to Mark Ronson, she wrote the famous title track of *Back to Black* with remarkable speed, including the lyrics. "The really respectful thing about the movie is you are reminded why she was famous in the first place—she was a genius, that's the stuff even I can forget. I forget that when I played her the piano chords to 'Back To

227   "Mitch Winehouse on Amy the Film: 'I told them they were a disgrace. I said: You should be ashamed of yourselves," by Emine Saner, TheGuardian. com, 05/01/2015.
228   *Amy* (Kapadia, 2016)

Black,' she wrote the lyrics in an hour... I was blown away; people just don't write lyrics like that any more. On 'Rehab' as well, she wrote those lyrics in two hours and they're so honest. Whoever thought there'd be a pop record about preferring to listen to Donny Hathaway than going to rehab, in 2006? Hers were the most open, honest lyrics you're ever going to hear on pop radio." [229]

Again, a paradox: all the while she was producing great music, she was drinking, and had begun to order large amounts of food, eat it, and excuse herself to purge afterwards. This was the first time the people she worked with began to suspect she had an eating disorder.

Still, her personal problems were outshone by a seemingly bottomless well of songwriting and singing talent. Again, we must remember that Winehouse wrote her own songs at a time when very few pop singers were expected to write a single line of their own. Winehouse was an outlier, and she stood out in just the right way. The accolades, financial success, and critical acclaim began to roll in. It was the right place and the right time for her particular jazz-pop-blues sound and her charmingly edgy character, which was not, really, a character at all; she was showing her bare, naked self from the get-go. The turning point that Shymansky predicted had arrived, and with it, the paparazzi hordes that would no longer leave her alone. "She was almost embarrassed by the fact that she was doing so well," recalled Mos Def, "She was just like, 'What am I

---

229   "Mark Ronson: Amy Winehouse Documentary Showcases 'Genius' Singer," by Daniel Kreps, RollingStone.com, 07/07/2015.

supposed to do in this space?' "

Against her wishes, her personal life became the subject of tabloid fascination, which was, by her own admission, the part of making music she wanted the least to do with. She said she was only good for "making tunes," [230] and merely wanted time and space to do so. Her relationship with Blake Fielder-Civil reignited, and was further plagued with arguments. Fielder-Civil has since admitted that he was the one that introduced her to heroin, and other hard drugs. "I'd enjoyed it. It completely eradicates any sort of negative feelings," Fielder-Civil said, "And then Amy tried it with me. And it just got a grip of both of us really quickly from then." [231]

The critical acclaim and the fan response to "Rehab," especially, is bittersweet, and cuts to the core of the relationship between a troubled artist and the public that loves what art comes from their trouble. Of course, it is a great song, but there is darkness behind it, like so many great songs. At the time, the song and its album, *Back to Black* were received with the dark humor with which they were sung. People laughed with her, rebelled with her, and simultaneously marveled at the classic jazz-blues-pop vocal style and the strange, acidic lyrics that were all so unlike her contemporaries. Her confident audacity, her tattoos, and the loud, beehive hairstyle (and, of course, that voice) turned her into a charismatic pop culture symbol of rebellion. However, it should be painfully obvious for anyone familiar with the term

230   *Amy* (Kapadia, 2016)
231   Ibid.

"enabler," of the Alcoholics Anonymous variety, why it is problematic for a song written about her refusal to go to rehab to become her biggest identifying hit. The world, quite literally, decided together to validate a moment that was probably a poor health decision, tacitly encouraging her to reject help. If I was in her shoes, it would be hard not to draw a clear correlation there: "Reject rehab," the fans seem to say, "reject help, and your songs will be bigger, and better, and more loved." It's a very dangerous concept to ingrain in someone's mind, someone who might need help. There is no rule that charisma must always scale with health or vitality. It seemed to be the opposite in this case; people seemed to warm themselves on the fires of her burning personal life, which she stoked and turned into songs. Her problems, raw and real as they were, were taken as half-serious at the time, and we all collaborated in that interpretation because she was clever, sarcastic, and sung and wrote so very well.

Adding gasoline to this fire, Winehouse and Fielder-Civil were married soon after the album broke big. The tabloids would continue to follow her, and report ravenously when she began performing visibly drunk, sometimes unable to finish, if she showed up at all.

Winehouse's first overdose happened in 2007, on an astounding mix of "heroin, cocaine, ecstasy, ketamine, whisky and vodka." [232] In a well-worn pattern we've seen from the others on this list, this hospitalization delayed a North American tour, and foreshadowed the events to

232   "Amy Winehouse," Biography.com.

come. She would later show up to gigs highly intoxicated, once booed from the stage for being unable to sing, remember lyrics, or even the names of her bandmates.[233]

An attempted intervention by close friends, including Shymansky, was undermined by the constant paparazzi presence and yet another, unwanted visit from Fielder-Civil at a critical moment. "Within hours, there were *Sun, Mirror, News of the World* journalists booked up in every room. Every single conversation that happened was in *The Sun* and *The Mirror*. Fuck knows if they were hacking the phones. And there's pictures of all of us sat outside, the doctor's just been round to check her blood, Blake's managed to get into her bedroom, and the next checkup the doctor's found out she's got heroin in her blood again." [234]

Her new manager reassured her distraught friends, who had no idea Winehouse had ever done heroin, that "lots of professionals" [235] function perfectly well on the drug. Anything, it seemed, was permissible if it would allow her to continue her planned tour in America, even in light of the seizure she had experienced and a warning from the doctor that another would kill her.

Many tried to intervene and get her back into treatment, including friend, comedian Russell Brand (b. 1975), but at every turn Fielder-Civil seemed to follow like a shadow. The management acquiesced, against all

233   "This Amy Winehouse footage is shocking!" Heat.co.uk, 19/06/2011.
234   *Amy* (Kapadia, 2016)
235   Ibid.

reason and medical advice, to allowing the couple to go to rehab, together, as a sort of compromise. During treatment, Fielder-Civil would playfully tease Winehouse on home-video about the irony of her current situation, given the lyrical content of her biggest song.

Shortly after the rehab stint, they relapsed together. Winehouse would soon be documented by the ever-present tabloids having very public scuffles with her husband. He would be photographed with numerous scratches on his face, and her with smeared and running eyeliner. Fielder-Civil was arrested for alleged bribery that same year. Needless to say, separating from her "other half" sent Winehouse further into despair. As the saying goes, she seemed to not be able to live with him or without him.

As the woman herself fell ever further into an abyss, her album went platinum multiple times over. She was nominated for a Mercury Prize and two Brit awards, and collected half-a-dozen Grammy awards (at the time tying Beyoncé's record for most Grammys won in a single show, entering the Guinness Book of World Records), one of which was presented to her by her hero, Tony Bennett. *Back to Black* was the second-highest-selling album in the world by 2008.[236] In the midst of all this, she took a close friend aside during the Grammys celebration, almost immediately after her win was announced, and whispered to her, "This is so boring without drugs." [237]

---

236   "Amy Winehouse," Biography.com.
237   *Amy* (Kapadia, 2016)

By this point, she had lost an extreme amount of weight.[238] She was diagnosed with emphysema and irregular heartbeats (a result of smoking and crack cocaine use). After her husband was sentenced to a rehab facility again, the couple finally filed for divorce.

"It was like a feeding frenzy," Shymansky said, "Suddenly it was cool to crack jokes about a bulimic's appearance or her drug addictions." [239] The analogy of a feeding frenzy could not be more apt, especially if you see the footage of the piranha swarms of paparazzi slamming into her, sometimes literally, as she leaves her apartment looking frail. Given its context, the relentless flashes and shouts are difficult to watch, as they visibly wear on a fragile and paranoid young woman. At the time, however, even I remember seeing her believably portrayed as just another "crazy celebrity," one who acts out and dresses colorfully. That she was a young woman who needed help seemed to escape all of our minds. She became a punchline on late-night talk shows in both the UK and the US.

To escape the noise, Winehouse left for St. Lucia with her father and some friends, and though she was blessedly free of cocaine and heroin, she substituted it for even heavier drinking.

After this short respite, she got to do a live studio duet with that aforementioned idol, Bennett. She was distraught and hyper self-critical, and blushing like the super-fan she was during the tapes of these sessions, but

---

238   "Amy Winehouse Bio," *Rolling Stone* editors, RollingStone.com.
239   *Amy* (Kapadia, 2016)

Bennett had nothing but glowing things to say about working with her.

"The most famous artists I've ever met are the most nervous before they hit that stage," Bennett said. "No matter how much you feel it, you want to feel it even more so that it becomes an honest recording. And that's what Amy had." [240]

Perhaps this could have been a turning point for Winehouse. She had flown a high middle finger to everyone who tried to get her clean. However, this time, Winehouse had made her next album's intentions known early: She wanted to do a series of more positive, love-oriented songs. "I like that idea. I don't want to do another record of 'screw you' songs," she told the *Irish Times*, "I am a very romantic person." [241] This could have been the moment to show the world that her voice, her talent, was enough—she could be clean, and continue on. She began feeling creative again, and had good periods where even her drinking had relaxed. She made a lot of noise about new albums, and collaborations with Mos Def and Questlove (b.1971). However, this was not to last. The pressures of a new tour branded as her "big comeback," and the pressure from the public to keep going back to her star-making *Back to Black* album (and all the emotional history it symbolized for her) drove her to the bottle again.

By the time of her death, which was from alcohol

---

240   Ibid.
241   "Amy Winehouse's 'Back to Black': 10 Things You Didn't Know," by Maura Johnston, RollingStone.com, 10/27/2016.

poisoning and the negative health consequences of her eating disorder, the world's focus had been split in half. Half of the attention was on her comeback and her talent. The other half, the more energetic and ravenous half, was focused squarely on the mire of her drug and alcohol addiction. Extreme public attention, that microscope onto her personal life with which she had always been uncomfortable, was a symbol of the macabre inverse relationship between success and tragedy. The widespread encouragement of this pattern is baffling; shortly after her death, she broke yet another Guinness Book record for most singles by a woman to chart in the UK at the same time.[242] After she passed, her brother suggested that bulimia, in addition to her drug and alcohol addiction, was a major factor in her deterioration.[243]

Near the end, her bodyguard Andrew Morris remembers her confiding in him, "If I could give it back, just to walk down that street with no hassle, I would." [244] It's a sobering quote, and illustrates just how psychologically damaging the tabloid microscope can be to people who are not prepared for it.

I spoke to Phil "Spiky" Meynell, a close friend of my son who was featured in the Oscar-

---

242   "Rihanna, Lady Gaga and Adele break World Records with Digital Music Sales," by Guinness World Records, GuinnessWorldRecords.com, 09/07/2012.
243   "Growing Up With My Sister Amy Winehouse," by Elizabeth Day, TheGuardian.com, 06/23/2013.
244   *Amy* (Kapadia, 2016)

winning documentary *Amy*, and was a central player
in the Camden rock 'n' roll scene in which Winehouse
immersed herself. He shared his firsthand perspective of
what Winehouse was really like, as a person and a friend.
The resulting account paints the picture of a girl who
was emotionally fragile, but by virtue of her very fragility,
seemed more capable of compassion for others:

> I remember, she was always the funny girl
> in the group. She accidentally ended up on the
> rock 'n' roll scene in Camden purely because
> of her location. I remember she always wanted
> to make you laugh and be the showman to her
> friends—but when it came to romance, she
> wanted to be little and shy, demure and looked
> after. She kind of let you be her boss, but she
> also let you *know* she was letting you. She longed
> for structure in her life but never got it. Her
> biggest fear was being alone and, sadly, that's
> how it ended.
>
> Reality didn't seem real anymore [after her
> big break]. She would shoplift small things as she
> got papped and shopkeepers would let her do it,
> and she couldn't believe it. She wanted someone
> to say no, and they never did. She loved music
> and loved jazz, but she thought she was a fraud.
> She would always say, 'What happens when they
> find out I'm putting this voice on?'
>
> She dreamed of having a family, and
> would always think of others before herself. She

would mother everyone that she was around. Whenever we would hang she would always sleep in our bed, on the end of the bed like a cat. She never seemed to want to be alone, and I think she still craved the security of being a kid again, with mum and dad still together. I remember she wanted to give up concentrating on her music toward the end and wanted a family, and to start a label and give opportunity to other artists and collaborate. She always wanted others to shine. She was a very smart, very clever, funny girl with a love for music. Sadly, she grew to fame in the wrong era of London when everyone—and I mean *everyone*—did heroin. She was an all-or-nothing girl… if this was 10 years on, she would be addicted to being healthy and working out, for sure, like everyone is now. I think she was a victim of drug trends more than anything.

She didn't really overdose in the regular sense of the word. She was just very small and fragile and was sober for a long time and fell off the wagon. The way she was sleeping cut off her breathing. If someone was sleeping next to her, they could have helped, but the worse thing for me is that she was alone.

Though her most famous album was inspired by a toxic relationship, I feel a strong sense of anger toward the system of enablers around someone like

Winehouse, especially toward her ex-husband, who participated in the "drug trend" that Meynell describes. It undermined the real friends that tried to help her. It takes a certain kind of person to deliberately introduce a very young, vulnerable person to hard drugs, and it should not be controversial to lay responsibility, at least in part, to people like Fielder-Civil when we mourn our artists. When I have been outspoken and made publicly crude or plain deplorable statements because of my misunderstanding, my dehumanizing of addicts, I was roundly called out for it, and rightfully so. I think we should expect the same response to actual enablers—dismissal and ridicule—because peer pressure causes people to make choices that harm them. Enablers are the demons on artists' shoulders, and many of these artists grow up already feeling isolated and vulnerable, teetering and ready for a push into the abyss. These enablers, in my opinion, are the ones that cause us to lose our artists sooner than we should.

Like Joplin before her, I believe Winehouse's voice, her lyrics, and her work in general is frankly more important than her various ailments, her problems, or her relationships. That voice existed in every phase of her personal health, before and after heroin, and so the voice belonged to her. She begged the public, throughout her life, to focus more on the songs, the brilliant songs, that she wrote in an age where writing one's own material was rare. Even as we attempt to understand what drove her as a human being, perhaps we should oblige her request.

Notable Mentions

Alan "Blind Owl" Wilson
1943 – 1970
Ron "Pigpen" McKernan
1945 – 1973
Jonathan Brandis
1976 – 2003

> "I don't know how many
> *Born Frees* I have
> left in me. I can't just
> keep playing kids."
>
> —JONATHAN BRANDIS[1]

1   "For Jonathan Brandis, now in 'Born Free,' play time is almost over,"
by R.D. Heldenfels, *The Philadelphia Inquirer*, 04/26/1996.

Notable Mentions

The 27 club has an official Mount Rushmore of names, those monumentally well-known figures we have discussed already. But there are many more that fall into the category, depending on how you define the club itself.

As I've said before, there is something a little queasy about talking about "membership" in the "club" this way. It seems to make some sort of achievement out of death at a certain age, and that is something I can't abide, no matter my attempts to put my judgment aside for this project. Needless to say, the figures themselves would likely not consider their own passings, most of which are accidental or a result of serious hardship, as badges or trophies, and neither would their loved ones.

So, keeping that in mind, the following are a list of "Notable Mentions," followed by a list of "Almost 27s," meaning artists and figures who are slightly less well-known but also fit the pattern, in their lives and their deaths, described by the vague notion we call the "27 club." This includes figures that are household names themselves, as well as less famous figures. It also includes more famous figures that passed very close to, but not exactly at, age 27.

Other examples of "club" members include Kristen Pfaff, bassist for Hole and close friend of Kurt Cobain and Courtney Love, who died of a heroin overdose just two months after Cobain's suicide. Also on the Seattle grunge scene was Mia Zapata, lead singer of the Gits who was raped and murdered on her way home from a gig. Her influences, true to type, had been jazz greats like Bessie Smith, Billie Holiday, and Sam Cooke.[245]

Richey Edwards, guitarist and lyricist of the Manic Street Preachers, went missing at the age of 27 in 1995 and was finally presumed dead in 2008. Edwards' death is suspected to be a suicide, but his family still have hope of establishing a definite narrative as of this year.[246] Peter de Freitas, the drummer of Echo & The Bunnymen, died in a motorcycle accident at 27 in 1989, and, more recently, Kim Jong-hyun, also 27, lead vocalist for K-Pop band Shinee, died by suicide, stating in a note: "I'm broken from the inside." [247]

There are plenty of other people who

---

245   "Mia Zapata," Wikipedia.com, accessed: 06/26/2018.
246   "Richey Edwards' family find "vital new evidence" in the case of missing Manic," by Andrew Trendell, NME.com, 02/09/2018.
247   "Jonghyun's suicide note reveals pressures of fame, depression that 'consumed' him," by Amy B. Wang, WashingtonPost.com, 12/19/2017.

were "Almost 27" too. Heath Ledger and James Dean in the world of film, who died at 28 and 24 respectively. In the world of music, there is punk icon Sid Vicious, frontman of the Sex Pistols, who committed suicide at just 21. In the world of rap, hip hop, and R&B, there are many notable names who never made it close to 27: Tupac Shakur, who was murdered at 25, Notorious BIG, who was fatally shot at 24, and Aaliyah, who died in a plane crash at just 22 years old.

It should go without saying, I hope, that the chosen adjective, "notable," refers specifically to their lives, not to their young deaths. Their ages at death are a bit of trivia, only useful for categorization purposes. They should not be the aspect that makes them notable. I think it is important to reiterate this intention clearly, lest I succumb to the same macabre romanticism I criticized in the introduction.

Alan "Blind Owl" Wilson

There are a few figures on this list that can claim the coveted title of blues aficionado, and Canned Heat's quiet, introverted guitarist and singer Alan "Blind Owl" Wilson is probably the most legitimate of all (besides Robert Johnson himself, of course). At the time, and still now in some circles, being a white guy that can actually play the blues with proper feeling, who knows his stuff and can cite blues scripture, is a coveted badge of honor. There's a feeling of authenticity, and perhaps artistic redemption, that comes along with being white and accepted by black blues heroes, no doubt due to the horrific racial history associated with the genre's creation. Ron "Pigpen" McKernan of the Grateful Dead, as we will discuss later, astounded his bandmates with his encyclopedic knowledge of blues.

But the only other figure on this list with better blues credentials must be Wilson, though this was not immediately obvious from his appearance or demeanor. Wilson was white and bookish, a music major at Boston University—more like a music historian or archivist than a rock star. So, how does Wilson fare against his contemporaries, all of whom (including the Stones) boasted of their love of blues and their connection to this music genre that came from a culture outside of them? How could the academic Wilson hope to compete? Perhaps by being featured on the blues records themselves, before his big break? Perhaps by stepping in, and, almost single-handedly, resuscitating the career of one of the all-time, primordial roots music heroes? Yeah, that'll do it.

Obsessively collecting records and writing articles and college theses about his favorite blues figures (Skip James ((1902–1969)), Muddy Waters, Charley Patton, Robert Johnson) was not enough for young Wilson. He actually managed to "[track] down forgotten blues pioneer Son House and [...] taught the old man 'how to play like Son House again.' House's 1965 album *Father Of The Delta Blues* featured Wilson on guitar and harmonica, and the pair would play together again in subsequent years."[248] How many fans can truly say they helped revive their hero's career?

Jamming and becoming a collaborator with Robert Johnson's legendary teacher is only one story. He also played with Mississippi John Hurt (c.1892–1966), Skip James (his vocal hero, the eerie falsetto of which he would go on to emulate with Canned Heat), and a handful of other forefathers of blues.[249]

When Canned Heat formed, they would go onto play the Monterey Pop Festival and Woodstock, unknowingly on the bill with more than one musician who would eventually share Wilson's age of death. Significantly, the band name itself was a drug reference: "'Canned Heat' was a nickname for Sterno, the ethanol and methanol-based cooking fuel that poor folks drank in order to get high, with often-fatal

248   "Canned Heat: The Twisted Tale of Blind Owl and The Bear," by Max Bell, LounderSound.com, 12/20/2014.
249   "Al Wilson (musician)," Wikipedia.com, accessed: 06/01/2018.

results. Wilson and Hite didn't know it at the time, but the lethal origin of their name would prove bitterly ironic," [250] writes Max Bell.

Wilson was another figure that seemed to live within a perfect storm of bad influences, from inside and outside of his control. He apparently struggled with major depressive disorder, and joined a band (like many others) that was notorious for its drug use—a combination that rarely seems to end well. "Like many in the 27 club, he was estranged from his family; he lacked confidence and suffered from depression. One of his eccentric habits was sleeping outdoors, as he did at vocalist Bob Hite's house in Los Angeles on the last night of his life." [251] According to Wilson himself, who was an avid environmentalist, this was a way to feel closer to nature.

Wilson's final record with Canned Heat would be yet another collaboration with one of his blues icons, John Lee Hooker (c.1912–2001), on the album *Hooker 'n Heat*—an effort to jam with a hero and also to give back to him. Hooker "wasn't exactly living in obscurity, [but] he wasn't benefiting monetarily from the wave of blues-influenced rock that was currently in vogue, either—at least not until Hooker 'n Heat," [252] said Jeff Giles. The album should have been a true moment of validation for Wilson; not only did he get to jam, yet again, with one

---

250   "Canned Heat: The Twisted Tale," Bell, LouderSound.com, 2014.
251   "The 27 Club: A Brief History," by *Rolling Stone* editors, RollingStone. com, 11/12/2013.
252   "That Time Canned Heat and John Lee Hooker Made 'Hooker 'N Heat,'" by Jeff Giles, UltimateClassicRock.com.

of the artists that inspired him to pick up an instrument in the first place, but his hero was caught on tape acknowledging Wilson's legitimacy, style, and dedication to the genre. "John Lee Hooker is heard wondering how Wilson is capable of following Hooker's guitar playing so well. Hooker was known to be a difficult performer to accompany, partly because of his disregard of song form. Yet Wilson seemed to have no trouble at all following him on this album. Hooker concludes that "you [Wilson] musta been listenin' to my records all your life." [253]

Wilson, meanwhile, was deprived some of the euphoria he rightly deserved after jamming and recording with his hero. Unfortunately, clinical depression does not always respond logically to good fortune, and Wilson's had worsened to the point that he had been "spending his nights at a psychiatric facility while the album was being tracked." [254] Wilson had tried to commit suicide unsuccessfully in the preceding months, and the album would not be released until after Wilson's death of barbiturate overdose.

It is hard to point a finger when you get into the details this way. Who is responsible for denying Wilson his happiness? Surely we cannot blame the man himself for having clinical depression. Then, do we blame those who gave him the drugs? Or, would he have eventually self-medicated anyway without the peer pressure, to relieve himself of the torture of his condition? It's simply not possible to know what could have made the difference.

253   "Al Wilson (musician)," Wikipedia.com.
254   "That Time Canned Heat," Giles, UltimateClassicRock.com.

Canned Heat, meanwhile, would soldier on without their blues scholar, and Wilson's heroes, John Lee Hooker and Son House, would, thanks to Wilson's efforts, enjoy access to an audience they had previously been denied.

Ron "Pigpen" McKernan

I don't remember who said it first, but it has been said that there is no such thing as a casual KISS fan. You are either indoctrinated, fully, into the aptly named "KISS Army," or you are a civilian. There is, rarely, an in-between. We've been lucky enough to foster a cultish devotion in our fans (or as I like to call them, our bosses, since we really do work for them), which has earned them this infamous nickname. There is even a coat of arms that represents them, like a militia or a biker gang. The KISS Army has conventions, clubs, and a culture of their own, independent of us, and has blossomed into something we never could have imagined.

There are few other acts in history that have been able to claim the same accomplishment—fans that have created a subculture, and coined terms for themselves in this way. The Beatles, as always, are the best example of this, stoking their notorious "Beatlemania" everywhere they went, like the true British royal family. There is Jimmy Buffett (b.1946), with his "Parrot Heads." Even, to take some contemporary examples, Justin Bieber, with the tween (and sometimes, strangely, older) "Beliebers."

And then there are the Grateful Dead, with their devoted "Deadheads."

The Grateful Dead's fan base really is something to behold; a puzzlingly devoted following that seems extraordinary whether or not you happen to like the music itself. Deadheads would, and still do, follow the band wherever they decide to play, going from show to show to show, city to city, state to state, as though on a never-ending pilgrimage. This is the band that Ron McKernan founded.

Jerry Garcia nicknamed Ron McKernan "Pigpen," possibly as a reference to his personal hygiene, and the two played together in a number of bands before eventually founding the Grateful Dead.

McKernan shares biographical similarities with many of the more well-known names on this list. Like Winehouse, his background in music came from his family, his father being "one of the first white R&B disc jockeys on a black station,"[255] which likely informed his tastes.[256] He was apparently "a veritable encyclopedia of bluesology,"[257] and thus it should come as no surprise that he and fellow blues fanatic Janis Joplin shared some romance and a close camaraderie. McKernan knew his stuff, and not just the obvious choices like Robert Johnson's "Cross Roads." He knew obscure, esoteric selections that only a true fetishist could recall, and this steered the early Grateful Dead's musical choices.[258]

Like Brian Jones, he was by many accounts the heart and soul and original founding member of a blues-centric group that would outlive him with a more

255   *Living with the Dead: Twenty Years on the Bus with Garcia and the Grateful Dead*, by Rock Scully (Cooper Square Press, NY: 2001)
256   "Artist Biography: Ron "Pigpen" McKernan," by Rachel Sprovtsoff, AllMusic.com, accessed: 06/01/2018.
257   *Living with the Dead*, Scully (2001)
258   Ibid.

famous, flagship front man. He would see his band drift
away from him, becoming alienated by his refusal to
adapt to new material and by the figure of guitarist Jerry
Garcia (1942–1995), as well as McKernan's own heavy
drinking. In the end he would watch the band take a
different musical direction, away from the blues roots he
originally intended.[259] "In the original earliest incarnation
of the band […] Pigpen played a large role because he
was the one with the most musical knowledge. He *was* the
Grateful Dead, according to Garcia." [260]

Also like Jones, his addiction would eventually
hamper his productivity, and would cause his band to hire
new members to pick up the slack. Like Morrison near
the end, McKernan's drug of choice was alcohol, unlike
his bandmates who, with all of the other counterculture
figureheads of the time, favored psychedelics. The
difference between McKernan and his bandmates can,
in a way, be summed up by the differences between
these substances: McKernan wanted blues and gospel,
the grounded classics, as the Dead were leaning toward
psychedelia, the weird, the spacey, the new.

In the end, McKernan's heavy drinking proved
too much. His deteriorating health prevented him from
touring, and he separated from the band and died in 1973
of an internal blood hemorrhage around the liver.[261]

Like his sometime romantic partner (and, sadly,

---

259   "45 Years Ago: The Grateful Dead's Ron 'Pigpen' McKernan Dies," by
Dave Swanson, UltimateClassicRock.com.
260   *Living with the Dead*, Scully (2001)
261   "'Pigpen' McKernan Dead at 27," by *Rolling Stone* editors,
RollingStone.com, 04/12/1973.

fellow member of this list) Joplin, McKernan was known to his friends as gentle and sweet, despite his biker-gang-aesthetic way of dressing. "'He was a warm, lovable cat,' says Dr. Eugene Schoenfeld. 'Unlike many rock & roll stars, he never projected an image of skulking evil.'" [262]

To this day, the band McKernan started with Garcia remains a subcultural fixation, an emblematic identity that one can still find on bumper stickers and t-shirts and college dorm room walls. Much has been made of an ever-increasing pantheon of celebrities and public figures that count themselves Deadheads, including such bizarrely eclectic names as Ann Coulter, John Belushi, Barack Obama, John Mayer, Nancy Pelosi, Tony Blair, Whoopi Goldberg, and George R.R. Martin, among many others. [263] [264]

As The Grateful Dead's official website puts it:

> Starting a rock band was actually Ron McKernan's idea, and he was its first front man, delivering stinging harmonica, keyboards, and beautiful blues vocals in the early years of the Warlocks/Grateful Dead. Nicknamed "Pigpen" for his funky approach to life and sanitation, he was born into a family that was generally conventional, except for the fact that his (Caucasian) father was an R&B disc jockey.

262   Ibid.
263   "Deadhead," Wikipedia.com, accessed: 06/01/2018.
264   "Ann Coulter: I'm a Grateful Dead Fan For Life," by Ann Coulter, Billboard.com, 06/24/2016.

And that sound put Pig's life on the rails of the blues from the time he was 12. Liquor, Lightnin' Hopkins, the harmonica and some barbecue— it was an unusual life for a white kid from San Carlos, but it was Pig's life. And the hard-drinkin' blues life began to catch up with Pig by the very early '70s. He played his last show with the band in 1972, and on March 8, 1973, he died of internal hemorrhaging caused by his drinking.[265]

Pigpen was a blues aficionado who the mob might say, "lived fast, died young"; I prefer to say that he never got to share what he could have with the world.

---

265   "Ron 'Pigpen' McKernan," Dead.net, accessed: 06/27/2018.

Jonathan Brandis

The success of the new Stephen King's *It* adaptation comes as no surprise to those of us who remember the original, with the great Tim Curry's terrifyingly camp-creepy performance. This original, of course, also featured then-teen idol Jonathan Brandis. Unknown to many at the time, Brandis, though a heartthrob, would probably have preferred the steady longevity of Curry's career to his own intense flash in the pan.

The term heartthrob, here, is not used frivolously—Brandis reportedly received over 4,000 gushing fan letters a week at the height of his fame, much of them from swooning young girls.[266] He started early, and began modeling at two and acting at four, diving into show business before his brain was developed enough even to begin making permanent memories, let alone to consent to a show business career.

He landed a recurring spot on the soap opera *One Life To Live* at six years of age, and soon was a regular guest on bigger scripted shows like *The Wonder Years*, *Murder, She Wrote*, and *Full House*.[267]

Brandis' starring feature debut was in the still fondly remembered *Never Ending Story* sequel, *The Next Chapter*, and the *It* miniseries was the same year—the latter garnering him the first whiffs of the critical acclaim

266   "Jonathan Brandis: How Life After Teen Stardom Can Take a Wrong Turn," by Amy Nicholson, LAWeekly.com, 11/12/2013.
267   "seaQuest DSV' Actor Jonathan Brandis Dead at 27," *CNN* editors, CNN.com, 11/24/2003.

he seemed to crave. His momentum, at this point, must have seemed inevitable. It was only a matter of time until he would transition into a full-fledged star.

This transition took the form of a role on a Stephen Spielberg-helmed sci-fi television series called *seaQuest DSV,* earning him a Young Artists Award and propelling him onto numerous covers of *Tiger Beat* magazine, and onto the bedroom walls of thousands of teens across the country.

This is another one of those situations where, from the outside, one would be hard-pressed to find something wrong with Brandis' situation. He was living the dream, and even if that dream only had a brief shelf life, surely it was better to have experienced it and lost it than never to have experienced it at all. Brandis, however, did not seem to agree—his dream was slightly different.

"'I never perceived myself like this—a teen magazine kid," Brandis said. "As an actor, you just hope to continue working." [268] Though this line was said with a relatively light tone, his ambivalence about his situation comes through here.

In what must have seemed to Brandis like an abrupt turn, "*seaQuest* was canceled in 1996, just before Brandis turned 20, [and] the casting offers stopped." [269] Why his career went from feast to famine in such a short amount of time is anyone's guess. Perhaps the gatekeepers of Hollywood saw the *seaQuest* cancellation as confirmation that the young man could not carry a

268   "Jonathan Brandis: How Life After," Nicholson, LAWeekly.com, 2013.
269   Ibid.

show to term, or maintain audience interest once he had aged out of his teens. Whatever the reason, Brandis, who by this point had every reason to believe his time was coming, found himself a sudden *persona non grata*. Though he tried changing his appearance in subtle ways and pursuing more serious, adult roles, he found himself without any work at all for more than two years, with the exception of a small role in the Bruce Willis vehicle *Hart's War* in 2002, in which Brandis' part was mostly left on the editing room floor.[270]

A coming-of-age interview with Brandis from 1996 now seems, sadly, like it captured the last peak before the trough. The journalist depicts an upbeat young actor, newly 20, who is cheerfully ready to move on to more adult roles, and even onto writing and producing. Jennifer Mangan writes:

> It isn't just time to move; Jonathan feels it's also time to move on. On April 13, he turned 20, kissing teendom goodbye—and with it, he hopes, any last traces of the teen-idol image he was saddled with from working in moves like *Sidekicks* and *Ladybugs*. […] The actor, who has been in the business since he was 4, wants the next phase of this career to include work behind the camera, writing and directing TV shows and movies.[271]

270   Ibid.
271   Act 2, Scene 1" by Jennifer Mangan, *The Item*, 04/28/1996.

Brandis is often seen as emblematic of a certain kind of celebrity tragedy—that thing that happens when you give a very young kid an overdose of worldwide love and attention, and then abruptly take it away after they reach a certain age. The psychological effects of such a rejection seem easy to speculate about, and Brandis' story is not the only example. Amy Nicholson writes in *LA Weekly*:

> How many of those teen heartthrobs transitioned into adult stars? One. [Leonardo] DiCaprio acknowledged the cull in a 2010 interview with *Rolling Stone*. "My two main competitors in the beginning, the blond-haired kids I went to audition with, one hung himself and the other died of a heroin overdose," he said. The suicide is Brandis. The OD could have been any one of several.[272]

A year after *Hart's War*, Brandis hanged himself. An obituary at the time wrote:

> Maybe the problem was that in a town where appearance matters so much, former teen idol Jonathan Brandis still looked great. Sure, his friends knew that the star of the mid-'90s TV series *seaQuest DSV* was lonely and depressed about his extended career lull. They knew he

---

272   Ibid.

drank heavily, and he'd even "told people that he was going to kill himself," says one friend. But no one, it seems, took him seriously enough.[273]

If one Googles Brandis' name now, you see him listed in "clickbait" articles with cynical, unsympathetic titles like "Celebrities Who Died and You Didn't Even Notice." Even in death, it seems, we cannot seem to stop putting the pressure on this kid for not quite living up to the expectations we assigned to him—for not, essentially, staying as young as we preferred him. For the sudden stars like Brandis, courting a fickle teen demographic, it is easy to see how this warped point of view could actually convince someone that the only way to capture eternal youth is to die before you get too old. This, of course, is a mistake—death does not keep you young, it only keeps you young in the minds of others.

273   "A Teen Heartthrob Takes His Life," by *People* staff, People.com, 12/08/2003.

The Almost-27s

Otis Redding
1941 – 1967
Tim Buckley
1947 – 1975
and Jeff Buckley
1966 – 1997

Otis Redding

If the category is "artist's artist," then it is not
an exaggeration to say that Otis Redding stands a head
above the rest.

Like many of the above, young Otis was raised
among the sounds of blues, the legendary Sam Cooke,
and Little Richard, growing up in the latter's hometown
of Macon, Georgia. He was a choir singer as a young
boy, and this gospel influence can be found in his own
music and all the fractal branches of those he would
influence through the ages. His performances later in life
would be likened to the energy of the black church, with
his calculated use of delayed gratification, ad-lib, and
false endings during his high-energy performances.

A teenaged Redding would sing in the Douglass
Theatre talent show for a grand prize of five dollars,
and was disallowed for competing after winning 15
times in a row.[274]

He joined other artists' bands, first. Like Hendrix,
he played behind Little Richard in a backing band
called The Upsetters. This would not be Redding
and Hendrix's only correlation.[275] His foray into pop
music proper was thanks to a guitarist named Johnny
Jenkins (1939–2006); Redding would go with him to the
recording studio in case he got a chance to lay something
down himself. That opportunity came in 1962; Jenkins

274   "About," OtisRedding.com (official website), accessed: 06/01/2018.
275   "Otis Redding Bio," by *Rolling Stone* editors, RollingStone.com,
accessed: 06/01/2018.

was having an unproductive day, and there was some time left at the end of the session. So, Redding jumped in and recorded "These Arms Of Mine," a now-classic song that would propel Redding into the spotlight.

He would pen his own hits, and his incredibly emotional performing style would see him challenge James Brown's (1933–2006) dominance on the charts.[276] Once he reached the public eye, other members of this list, icons with plenty of fans of their own, became Redding fans. Janis Joplin herself would wait patiently for hours for him to appear in his three-night stint at the Fillmore in Philadelphia,[277] and the Rolling Stones would cover his song, "Pain in My Heart," and were by many accounts among "his greatest admirers." [278] Redding would write his own hits, and turn others' songs into his own signature hits. He would re-record and make a charting hit out of the Rolling Stones' "Satisfaction," as well as the Bing Crosby/Frank Sinatra popularized "Try and Little Tenderness," reversing the common order (black songs covered/popularized by white artists) of sonic cultural syncretization that was the norm at the time. The latter was hard won, in that the publishers were reportedly not a fan of Redding taking their song and recording it from a "negro perspective." [279] The irony of this statement

276   "Otis Redding Bio," RollingStone.com.
277   "Epic New Otis Redding Biography Sheds Light on the Singer's Life and Times," by Will Hermes, RollingStone.com, 08/02/2017.
278   "Otis Redding: The Crown prince of Soul is Dead," by Jann S. Wenner, *Rolling Stone*, 01/20/1968.
279   *Performance and Popular Music: History, Place, and Time*, by Janis Inglis (Ashgate, UK: 2016)

should weigh heavily on us, considering bands like The Beatles, the Stones, and later Led Zeppelin and… well, almost everyone, would make their fortunes by covering and feeling inspired by black blues artists. Needless to say, Redding covered the song anyway, and arguably eclipsed the original version of "Try a Little Tenderness," making the song his "signature." [280] I've always said the best revenge is success.

Success, too, found others who chose to cover Redding-penned tunes. Perhaps Aretha Franklin's best-known song, "Respect," is a Redding original, as is perhaps the best-known Black Crowes song, "Hard to Handle." [281]

Redding would expand his audience (especially his white audience) by performing at the Monterey Pop Festival, again sharing a venue with Janis Joplin (now a fellow performer), Jimi Hendrix (making that the second Little Richard backing band alumni on the stage), and Al Wilson with Canned Heat. If I was a superstitious man, I would probably take a long hard look at the Monterey Pop Festival—so many of these figures who died so close to the same age performed and found their creative footing there. According to *Rolling Stone*, Redding's set was particularly intense, so much so that Grateful Dead's Bob Weir (b.1947) remarked, "I was pretty sure that I'd seen God onstage." [282]

In only four years, songs we now consider to be true soul classics sprung from Redding's imagination.

280   "Otis Redding," Wikipedia.com, accessed: 06/01/2018.
281   "Otis Redding Bio," RollingStone.com, accessed: 06/01/2018.
282   "Epic New Otis Redding Biography," Hermes, RollingStone.com, 2017.

Strangely, none of his singles fared better than number 21 on the pop Top 40, until after he passed. According to music journalists and fans around the globe that recognize his greatness today, this was probably due to him being ahead of his time, or as the Rock & Roll Hall of Fame put it, "too intensely soulful for the mainstream market at the time." [283]

Redding wrote "(Sittin' on) The Dock of the Bay" with Steve Cropper shortly after Monterey Pop. The session was apparently more eclectic than his usual fare, as Redding was inspired in part by the chemical reaction of infiltrating and interacting with the hippie counterculture at Monterey, and by the release of *Sgt. Pepper's Lonely Hearts Club Band*.[284] The song was, apparently, somewhat of an afterthought "at the end of a long session. The whistling at the end came about, Cropper claims, because Redding forgot a vocal fadeout he had rehearsed before." [285]

Redding himself would not live to see the song's release. Six months after Monterey, a private jet, carrying Redding and the exceedingly young members of his band the Bar-Kays, crashed into Lake Monona in 1967.[286] Redding was 26.[287]

It seems strange on hindsight that in an interview

283   "Rock & Roll Hall of Fame Inductees: Otis Redding," RockHall.com, accessed: 06/01/2018.
284   "Epic New Otis Redding Biography," Hermes, RollingStone.com, 2017.
285   "Otis Redding Bio," RollingStone.com, accessed: 06/01/2018.
286   "Rock & Roll Hall of Fame Inductees: Otis Redding," RockHall.com.
287   "Epic New Otis Redding Biography," Hermes, RollingStone.com (2017)

that same year, on *American Bandstand* with Dick Clark, they happen to discuss plane troubles:

> **Dick:** "You know what always amazes me? Nothing ever ruffles you. You had a cat and a dog of a fight getting here. Do you travel so much [that it] doesn't ever bother you anymore?"
> **Otis:** "Well, Dick, I had real trouble this morning. I missed the plane."
> **Dick:** "But, you know, this man, he always arrives. Come rain, sleet or snow—like the postman, Otis Redding will be here." [288]

Once it was released posthumously, "(Sittin' On) The Dock of the Bay" quickly ascended to number 1 and stayed there for four weeks.

There is temptation, in cases like these, to credit Redding's first number 1 hit as a result of "making saints of the dead." As we've seen with Winehouse's story, artists' sales do tend to jump shortly after they pass away, and we've reviewed how we all, to lesser or greater degrees, love to rewrite history in our heads. But I just cannot bring myself to grant this credence when it comes to Redding's legacy; especially when it comes to that song. To this day, that song still…well. You know, it, don't you? Doesn't everyone? The proof is in the pudding, as they say.

Biographers have reportedly had trouble, for a

---

288   Dick Clark, Otis Redding, *American Bandstand*, 01/21/1967.

host of bizarre reasons, in trying to write a proper life story of Redding. One of these reasons: he was a nice guy. According to Alan Light in the *New York Times:*

> Jonathan Gould, author of the insightful Beatles history *Can't Buy Me Love*, ran up against the same limitations all these efforts have faced: The singer did only a couple of interviews, and there's a fundamental lack of tension in the life of a person who virtually no one will say a bad word about. "He wasn't just a magnificent talent," said his manager, Phil Walden. "He was a magnificent man." [289]

This saintly image is humanized somewhat in Gould's 2017 biography, *Otis Redding: An Unfinished Life,* which Light describes as "impressive" in both its "access to Redding's surviving family" and its "exhaustive research into Redding's early years as a performer."[290]

Even in situations like Redding's, in which the artist's death was clearly an accident that could have happened to anyone, there's a certain level of temptation to pull narrative tension out of places where it does not really exist. This stands as a kind of *reductio ad absurdum* that it is nothing other than a macabre fascination with death that draws certain people into these stories. Clearly, to die young is the

289   "Soul of the '60s: Otis Redding's Short Life and Long Reach," by Alan Light, *New York Times*, 06/02/2017.
290   Ibid.

point, for so many eager onlookers; it is the icing on the cake, that which makes a story dramatic. But Redding was just so *good* at what he did, I think it is a shame to partition any of our mental or emotional energy away from his actual catalog of work. Had he been alive today, those songs would not, in my view, occupy any other position than the one they currently do: as some of the greatest of all time, period. It is a good thing, I believe, to keep our eye on this ball, and with songs and a voice like Redding's, it is easy.

Tim Buckley and Jeff Buckley

If there is a case to be made that there is something strangely dangerous, or at least transient, about being a young musician, it is illustrated by the cases of Tim and Jeff Buckley. Though they do not fall exactly at 27, they are definitely within the statistical cluster that causes that character—the tragic young artist cut short in his prime—to thrive in the public imagination.

Tim Buckley and Jeff Buckley are both names that did not sell an enormous amount of records during their short lifetimes, but nevertheless are both considered (like Redding, on a smaller scale) "musician's musicians," meaning that many more successful artists cite them as significant artistic influences. Jeff Buckley, in particular, is considered by many to be one of the "greats" despite having only a single studio album to his name. His early death is lamented as the loss of a budding icon that had already surpassed his father and would have, possibly, gone on to fully capture the public eye in the long run, had he had the opportunity

Tim Buckley, in his day, owed his cult following (and paradoxically his lack of major success) to an extraordinarily eclectic taste and output. He weaved between genres without care, from folk to jazz to the more experimental ventures of his later career. Early on, he championed the folk and blues-influenced music of his day, which caught the eye of Elektra Records.[291] However, he later tossed that aside, uncomfortable with the uncredited liberties white artists took with their black influences, describing the genre (of which he was a part) as, "white thievery and an emotional sham." [292] He never seemed comfortable conforming to a niche, and it is the rare musician that can weather the whiplash of fans attempting to keep up with his genre-wandering whims. As *Rolling Stone* put it:

> Though likened to such L.A. song poets as Jackson Browne and gifted with an impressive, multi-octave voice, Buckley never quite achieved real stardom. He first won attention as a sensitive, almost fragile, writer and singer, but during the late Sixties he began to explore unstructured jazz vocals, sometimes singing onomatopoetically onstage for up to an hour.[293]

The folk fans could not abide his turn to psychedelia, and the hippies could not comprehend his abrupt turn to the avant-garde and experimental. Despite coming from his least accessible album, Tim Buckley's most well-known song is probably "Song to the Siren" from *Starsailor*.

As much as Tim Buckley seemed to want to be true to himself, his inability to find a consistent

291   "Tim Buckley," Biography.com, accessed: 06/10/2018.
292   *Blue Melody: Tim Buckley Remembered*, by Lee Underwood (Backbeat Books, US: 2002)
293   "Tim Buckley Dead at 28," by Judith Sims, *Rolling Stone*, 08/14/1975.

demographic for his work took a toll on him, and like so many on this list, he turned to substances. Some saw his death at age 28 as uncharacteristic—though he drank, he was not apparently as dedicated to hard drug culture as many of his contemporaries. Jim Fielder (b.1947), bassist for Blood, Sweat & Tears, said that Buckley "was great, in real good shape. It was one of the healthiest times of his life" [294] when he died. He did, however, struggle with frustration at best, and depression at worst, regarding the ups and downs of his career, and he had experimented with hard drugs at varying points in his life. Though he was in a good frame of mind near the end, others close to him framed his early passing as foreseeable: "He continually took chances with his life. He'd drive like a maniac, risking accidents," said his lyricist Larry Beckett. "For a couple of years he drank a lot and took downers to the point where it nearly killed him, but he'd always escape. Then he got into this romantic heroin-taking thing. Then his luck ran out." [295]

Tim Buckley's death is unique for this list in that the person responsible for granting him the drugs that would take his life was actually held accountable, to some extent, by the law: "Ten days later, Richard Keeling, a 30-year-old research assistant in the music department at UCLA, was arraigned on charges of second degree murder. Keeling allegedly furnished Buckley with the drugs that caused his death." [296]

---

294   Ibid.
295   "Tim Buckley: 'The High Flyer,'" by Martin Aston, *MOJO*, 06/1995.
296   "Tim Buckley Dead at 28," Sims, *Rolling Stone*, 1975.

Tim Buckley's marriage to Mary Guibert had lasted little more than a year, but resulted in Mary giving birth to Jeff Scott Buckley in 1966. Both parents quickly remarried afterwards. Mary and Jeff would not be invited to Tim's funeral.[297]

Young Jeff would, apparently, only meet his father once, three months before Tim's passing. His mother brought Jeff to one of his father's concerts. Of the encounter, Jeff Buckley recalled: "'I sat on his knee for fifteen minutes… He smiled the whole time. Me too.'"[298]

In his young household, his father was symbolically seen and not seen:

> Jeff was a smiley "little hippie kid" living in California's Orange County and answering to the name of Scott or Scotty Moorhead… Jeff's family would always refer to him as "Scotty" to his dying day, but a few months after he learnt of his father's death, Jeff informed his mother that he wanted to use the surname Buckley in his dad's honour. According to Browne, it wasn't until 1980 that he began to use his real first name, which he discovered after finding his birth certificate.[299]

When Jeff Buckley would come of age and finally release his own music, his acclaim was rather

297   "Life Story: Jeff Buckley, the Haunted Rock Star," by Marie Claire, NZ.Yahoo.com, 05/03/2013.
298   Ibid.
299   Ibid.

more immediate than his father's. Like his father, he seemed to dip his toes lightly in a wide, bizarre range of genres. What other artist could be said to be just as inspired by opera and cabaret music as they are by Led Zeppelin? Of the latter, Jeff Buckley was a huge fan, and this sentiment was returned by lead singer Robert Plant (b.1948) who, at a dinner party, told the young artist how much he enjoyed his album.[300]

Jeff Buckley was ambivalent about his mysterious father, who seemed to hang around at the margins of his life constantly. He would play sporadic gigs in clubs and cafés, but it was not until he was contacted to play a cover of his father's song at a Tim Buckley tribute concert that the world began to take notice. The assumption that Jeff had done the concert in order to launch his own career seemed to irk him considerably: "'This isn't a springboard, this is something very personal. It bothered me I hadn't been to his funeral. I used that show to pay my last respects," Jeff clarified. "I sacrificed my anonymity for my father, whereas he sacrificed me for his fame." [301]

After this, record executives and hordes of fans began crowding his café shows, and it wasn't long until a record deal was in the works and a tour was underway. Once again, ambivalence seems to be the key word to describe Jeff's relationship with his success: "How overwhelming can something be? This has been the most surreal year of joy and utterly satanic bullshit mixed

300   Ibid.
301   Ibid.

together," [302] he wrote to his fans.

Jeff had inherited his father's multi-octave vocal range and penchant for eclectic music, and was in constant comparison with his father once he arrived on the scene. Also, like his father, his drug use did not at first seem to be a problem:

> At 17 [...] his music was his life—no-one ever saw him drinking alcohol, smoking or taking drugs. "He was so pure," family friend Tamurlaine Adams told [biographer David] Browne. "He was hardly interested in women or sex. He was happy, but the sadness and melancholy was always there. [303]

However, when full-fledged fame reared its head, Jeff exhibited the same pattern as many others on this list—he started to become paranoid, and felt "anguish at the loss of his creative anonymity." [304] His ambivalence for his father's legacy transferred to an ambivalence about the music business, and all the (in his view) crass motivations of the cynical "suits" therein. He began to experience writer's block, the success and critical acclaim of his first album putting pressure on the young man to match or top it next time.

This is where Jeff Buckley's story veers away from many on this list. Though Jeff enjoyed tequila and

302   Ibid.
303   Ibid.
304   Ibid.

marijuana, it is unclear if Jeff's experimentation with substance would have become a problem in his life; the young man would not live long enough to find out, and unlike so many, substance abuse would not be even peripheral to his downfall.

His death, so near the age of his father's, would come as a seemingly random accident. On a trip to Memphis to write and record, during which it seems his writer's block was being cured (or at least abated), Jeff had decided on a whim to jump into the Wolf River, fully clothed, for a night swim—perhaps to celebrate:

> Minutes later, he was floating, singing Led Zeppelin's "Whole Lotta Love." [Jeff's friend Keith Foti] stayed ashore and, after moving a radio and guitar out of reach of the wake of a passing boat, looked up to realise that Jeff was gone.[305]

Buckley was reported missing, and many speculated that the young man had taken his own life. These spectators probably meant well, but these kinds of things are always delivered with a peculiar, juicy, tabloid tone, as though they are almost hoping-not-hoping that this young musician would conform to the pattern of self-destruction with which his fans were familiar, as it had befallen so many of his contemporaries and idols. It wasn't until his body was found on June 4th that "the autopsy confirmed that he had no illegal drugs in his

---

305   Ibid.

system, and his estate insists it was simply a tragic accident." [306] You can almost hear the disappointment of the gossip mags, and the biographers.

Jeff Buckley's well-known cover of Leonard Cohen's (1934–2016) "Hallelujah," found on his only album, *Grace*, climbed the charts posthumously, and remains an oft-covered and referenced arrangement in pop culture. Many consider Buckley's performance to be superior to its original, much like Nirvana's cover of David Bowie's "Man Who Sold The World" seemed to supplant its source material in the public imagination.

It is clear that Tim Buckley and Jeff Buckley's deaths are not, strictly speaking, a pattern of behavior. Despite all the articles that would romance Jeff's death as a "paternal prophecy" or "looming fate," it is, in fact, a coincidence. An eerie coincidence, perhaps, but a coincidence nonetheless, and diving into the nitty-gritty details of how Jeff passed reveals just how incidental it was. It is just these sort of anomalies that give rise to memes like the 27 club itself—that young musicians die young at a higher rate seems to suggest something almost supernatural about the careers they chose. But, sometimes things do just happen. Not every correlation is a Shakespearean tragedy that can be neatly tied together in narrative form, nor should it be. Life is messy and random and strange.

If any pattern is to be extrapolated, it is that

---

306   Ibid.

a tendency towards risk-taking behavior plays a part; people do hard drugs despite knowing their risks, and that fact often plays a part in the high, or so I've been told. Looked at through this lens, the Wolf River in which Jeff Buckley drowned was "known by locals to be a dangerous swimming spot,"[307] and perhaps jumping into a dangerous river at night gives someone who enjoys a thrill a sort of high of its own. His father reportedly enjoyed driving recklessly for the thrill. Perhaps they shared this proclivity for thrill-seeking. This, of course, is pure speculation—it is very likely that Buckley just wanted to go for a swim, and had no daredevil inclinations at the time of his death—and it should not be the point, in any case. Jeff Buckley himself would likely resent even the exercise of comparing or contrasting his death with his father's.

If we are to look at what Jeff Buckley and his father share, let it be their voices, their artistry, and the music they worked so hard to make. Let that be the final word. Go listen to the albums, and let your ears decide whether the fact that these men happened to have passed away young adds anything of value to their material. I submit that it does not, and the material stands on its own.

---

307   Ibid.

"People don't realize that worldwide attention, worldwide fame overnight, is a potential trauma if you are wired a certain way."

—DR. JAMES FALLON

The Science of 27:
An Interview with Dr. James Fallon

Though the intention of this book is to offer my perspective (as a fellow musician and a fellow public figure) on these stories, the best way to discern fact from urban myth is still cold, hard science. Science is the fire that illuminates the dark cave; it's why we are here and why we are able to make sense of things that don't seem to make any. And so we may ask, now that we've sifted through the data of their lives: scientifically, why did the people in the 27 club take this path, and why do so many others in similar situations take a different one? Did these people choose to go down a certain route for the same reasons, or is this pure coincidence?

A pattern many of these stories share is the strange (to me) concept that fame—true worldwide fame—was a burden to these people, not a comfort, in the end. I think this strikes many of us as puzzling. There are many more of us in the music industry that feel quite comfortable up here—myself for one—and many people around the world who believe that fame is something they would enjoy, for all the obvious reasons. Power, respect, and fortune—to frame these as a negative life event seems ludicrous. The sort of inner struggle that many of these figures went through is hard for someone like me to understand, and perhaps that is what makes these stories so fascinating to the average person. It seems counterintuitive that there would be a dark consequence to what most people would consider the best possible outcome in life. There is a shadow that such a bright light casts, and apparently there are only certain people that fall beneath this shadow, whether due to addiction, depression, or some other related suffering.

As it turns out, there are scientific reasons that this should be so, and scientific reasons for the existence of the 27 club in general.

For that, I defer to an interview my son conducted with his acquaintance, neuroscientist Dr. James Fallon, professor of psychiatry and human behavior and professor emeritus of anatomy and neurobiology at the University of California. He is also the author of *The Psychopath Inside: A Neuroscientist's Personal Journey into the Dark Side of the Brain*, where he comes to terms with his own family's neurological legacy.

Nick Simmons: Thanks for speaking with us. To start, what do you know about the idea of the 27 club, and what does science have to say about it?

James Fallon: Well, first of all, if you look at suicides, overdoses, and all that through the lens of age, you see a couple of things. The one thing to understand going in is how brain development works. The brain is not what you would call mature until you are about 25 or 26. That is important to know because people don't really show the symptoms of, let's say, schizophrenia, for example, usually until about 18 to 22. That's because those areas of the brain that are broken in schizophrenics don't mature until then. The machine doesn't break because, until then, there isn't a completed neural machine to break yet. So there are age onset disorders that have to do with brain development, and these can be anything from depression or anxiety to schizophrenia. So if you look at the disease onset maps of schizophrenia and depression, it's the mid- to late-20s. It's at a time when what's called "axon myelination," the connections and all those mood affecting neurotransmitters, become mature. It's at about 25 or 26.

    I've used this data in my own life; I am an advisor to the Pentagon on the subject of "war and cognition," and I've used this to argue that no person should go to war before they're 25, because they are so susceptible to stressors before that age depending on their genetics. In the context of war, this data is relevant to PTSD and depression. So, the first puzzle piece is at the brain level—you really get vulnerable, neurochemically, at certain ages, and the mid-20s is one of these peaks where if something is going to go wrong, it does tend to happen around that time.

NS: So, it's a cocktail of nature and nurture?

JF: That's correct. People don't realize that worldwide attention, worldwide fame overnight, is a potential trauma if you are wired a certain way. Some people, maybe a quarter, are not wired to handle that, and are probably going to fall apart in some way. And, just as early stressors are crucial factors to people who have the genetics and brain chemistry for psychopathy, as another example, the same is true for depression, hyper-sensitivity, and schizo-affective disorders. Early stressors, early traumas, or even just coming from intense family situations can make people develop personality disorders in response, if they have the genetics for it. Add to that someone who's naturally artistic—they tend to have a higher rate of being born into families with depression, alcohol, and substance abuse anyway, because of their genetics. But with addiction, sometimes, genetics become a behavioral thing as well, which is passed down to the next generation, in duel ways. In these sometimes intense families, these people with this perfect cocktail of genetic and behavioral influences tend to "show" in their mid-20s.

This is true about the general population, so now

think about how the small percentage of these people that reach worldwide fame are affected—that's just an extra stressor. The neuroscience of it makes a lot of sense.

Now, if you say, why do artists specifically have these higher rates? Why are "creatives" prone to this, generally speaking? Studies have shown that artists have a higher percentage of bipolar disorder, depression, and schizo-affective disorder. Creative people tend to score high in these tests. So here you've got a profession that tends to get those afflictions anyway. To understand this, you have to know that the frontal lobe is, loosely speaking, the enemy of creativity. The frontal lobe helps organize behavior, it's basically the function of the agent and manager for a lot of artists. The agent is like their walking, talking prefrontal cortex; they do all the frontal lobe functions—organizational matters, business stuff. So artists often have labile prefrontal cortexes, and this allows them to think out of the box, to be creative, to access that part of themselves. It goes hand in hand that way: prefrontal cortex issues are correlated with creativity.

The next step is to look at the epidemiology of it. The 27 club is a statistical myth; it's not actually the highest peak on that graph. The highest peak of death for musicians is actually in their mid-50s. If anything, it should be a 55 club or a 56 club, not a 27 club. The numbers are higher there. You could look that age up and you'd see a lot of names you would know there as well.

But, the mid- to late-20s is the first time you see a large spike, a fast rise. The frequency seems higher in comparison to earlier in life, in childhood. In their 20s, the frequency is higher even though the absolute rate is lower. And then it plateaus; there's no increase after the late-20s/early-30s until you see that next peak, where it begins to ramp up from about 45 to 55, and then that peak is much higher. Then, of course, it goes down from there. The epidemiology of it would not support this idea that 27 is an especially significant number in terms of deaths overall, but there's a way of looking at it that the late-20s is when the rate of change ramps up for the first time, so it feels like there's a special number there.

NS: So what about the fans? People react to this idea with a mixture of emotions, some romanticize it and some react negatively. Why is that? Why are people fascinated?

JF: I would say that the people looking most closely at this pattern, that are responding to it, especially right when it happens, are probably between 15 and about 25. They are young people who, like the famous people they are responding to, are very impressionable. They have the same problems as their heroes, and because these problems are rooted in environmental stressors, setting off brain chemistry that exists in a lot of young people, it's very immediate to these fans. The fans look at that and they recognize it because they feel this same vulnerability in themselves. The artists that are usually brought up in conversation are the tragic, intense deaths of monumentally popular stars. I think the fan base for artists like these is itself made up of very sensitive people, because they tend to be younger than 25 and they're very labile. It's the same sort of neurochemical moment in development (in the fans) reacting to an extreme version of itself (in the artists).

So that is what creates the illusion that 27 is especially significant. For a fan, it's like when you hit yourself in the elbow in the morning really hard, and then it seems to you like you're hitting yourself in that spot all day long. You usually do, of course, make contact there on your elbow throughout your day, but it's not usually sore, so you don't notice it unless you have that extra level of sensitivity in a certain area. There's a mental hypersensitivity there of the fans to certain conditions.

And of course there's the obvious: that there was a certain era where the stars were just larger than life, mythological even. I mean Hendrix and Joplin, these people were really out there, really the first of their kind. But then so were the Stones and The Beatles.

I gave a Chicago Ideas talk on this topic, on the correlation between mental disorders, especially depression and bipolar disorder, and art and creativity. It's about the neurological correlates of creativity, and about what puts people with these neurological correlates, many of them artists, at risk.

NS:　Then, what would you advise these at-risk groups, either artists or fans, to help them deal with these mental health and behavioral issues?

JF:　Well, the more you know about biological

psychiatry and psychology, the better. Knowing the fact that there are genetics involved, and that there's also traumatic triggers involved, is a start. Just knowing how it all works really helps.

If you have a trauma in your past, it puts you at risk for this stuff later—for suicide and depression and addiction. And it's not everybody. Some people are at risk for different things. But for however much genetics plays a role, there's always a trigger, and the trigger usually happens in your mid-20s.

But, even if a trigger does not appear, most of these things, if you have them, are going to surface eventually. People used to think schizophrenia was caused by environmental factors alone, which is not true. It's really a genetic thing, it's just that the event that triggers the first psychotic break in depression and schizophrenia happens to be environmental. And it'll often be around the time when you're in college and you go on break, you'll be 19 or 20, for example, and something will happen, some first young adult problem that you haven't experienced before. And then you'll have another one when your girlfriend leaves you later on, for example, a bad break-up or something like that. You know, these triggers can be pretty normal, pedestrian life events. It's not that it always happens; it just needs to stress a system with the right genetics, and that's when the symptoms of what already exists in the brain surface.

NS: That seems to fit a lot of these stories, because some of the things that really tormented people on this list were fairly common life struggles like divorce and high school bullying, but those struggles lead to more serious things like severe addiction and depression. It seemed that even before substances, a lot of these people were very sensitive to things that other types of people let run off their back.

JF: Exactly. You know when you have kids, you always see that one out of two of them will fall down the stairs and come up laughing. And then the other one just falls apart emotionally. So it's not the objective stimulus, it's how the stimulus affects different brains. So divorce, for example, some kids aren't bothered by it at all. It's sort of an inconvenience. It doesn't traumatize them. But other times, something as common as a divorce can be really traumatic for a sensitive kid, especially a kid who tends toward depression anyway. And neither is right or wrong—the old generation used to sort of shun this sensitivity, as in the case of Hendrix's father, which didn't help anybody. It's not good or bad to be hypersensitive, it's just a matter of different brain chemistry, in addition to early attachment, and how those symbiotic relational needs are met, to what degree, which is unique to each individual. And artists, generally speaking, are extremely sensitive by nature. And so, it gives them a lot of relative power but simultaneously makes them very vulnerable.

So, the advice I would give is, if you're a teenager or a preteen, and you really think that you're hypersensitive, you have meltdowns or you find yourself taking things harder, or if you did have an early problem when you were young or were traumatized in some way, you should get a good interview with a psychologist and get professional advice.

Today, we have the capability to do genetic tests to see if people have genes that make them susceptible to depression, schizophrenia, and even addiction. We're able to see into the brain that way. Psychiatrists are utilizing DNA tests combined with functional brain imaging and psychometrics to determine even which psychiatric medications or non-drug treatments work uniquely for their patients. Additionally, we did a study that cost 40 million dollars on late teens/early-20s kids, and we knew by going through brain scans who was going to become a smoking addict and who was not, and the accuracy of our predictions using those brain scans was remarkably high.

That's a huge misunderstanding, still, about addiction—you are born with a high potential for addiction, just like depression. You're born with that. So my best advice to people, in the arts or otherwise, is to know yourself. You can't tell just by looking at your parents, either, because you can have two normal parents but they can be both carrying genes that tend toward depression or addiction and you inherit the alleles, the forms of those genes, that make you vulnerable. So it's not like it has to be the parents themselves. They may just be the carriers.

And, also, if you find you are one of these people,

you should remember that these things are neither good nor bad. The same things that make you sensitive probably help make you creative.

NS: That's fascinating. It seems to me the error people make is they think that the suffering causes the art, when it seems like the truth is that the art and the suffering come from the same third cause, and that's your brain structure.

JF: That's right. It's a "common cause" dynamic. Now, most people familiar with my work know I have my own issues that I wrote a book about, and I revel in this knowledge, because it allows me to control my own responses, because I know what I'm watching out for. I know certain things are off balance in my brain, and I explain it to people, and I know what I'm sensitive to. People who do this, they can roll with the punches. It doesn't make life rosy, necessarily—there's no magic fix—but it makes life manageable, it makes you not fall apart.

NS: So there's a way to manage it without destroying your creativity.

JF: That's right. By having a more or less detailed knowledge of, first of all, the basic science of it. A lot of these figures were also very bright, especially Morrison, Basquiat, Cobain…these were really smart people, book-smart. The whole point of having a scientifically literate populace is to give laypeople enough information so that they can understand the dynamics of the forces that influence their lives. Genetic testing for susceptibility is expensive, but there are lots of other ways to find this stuff out about yourself. Being open and aware and eager to learn about your own brain and how people work is what matters.

We know that, to take drugs as an example, there's a whole slice of society who, genetically, can take a lot of drugs and never get addicted. This is something that the anti-drug lobby won't tell you, for fear of encouraging it, and then when kids inevitably find this out on their own and run into these people, they think the whole anti-drug thing is fraudulent. It'd be better to just educate everyone honestly. The addiction part has a lot to do with something called the corticotropin release hormone. There are a whole bunch of people who never get addicted. And then there are people who you know are most likely going to get addicted if they touch the stuff. Knowing what your brain is like, knowing who you are, neurochemically, learning enough science and psychology and knowing your family and yourself, gives you power. This is the sort of middle ground between "free love" and "just say no"—if you're going down a certain path, educate yourself about your brain beforehand, so you know what to guard against.

I hope, in this book, we motivate people to take a positive action, and knowing yourself, learning about your own brain, is one such action. But the responsibility is with the individual. Everybody is unique, and it can be fun and cathartic finding out what that uniqueness is.

Dr. James Fallon is Professor of Anatomy and Neurobiology at UC Irvine. He has achieved many accolades, including a Sloan Scholarship, a Senior Fulbright Fellowship, and a National Institutes of Health Career award. He is a Subject Matter Expert in the field of "cognition and war" to the Pentagon's Joint Command.

Final Thoughts

AVICII, AND THE FUTURE

In reviewing these stories and learning about these artists' histories, childhoods, environments, and learning about the underlying behavioral science and neuroscience, my eyes have been opened about things that never occurred to me before.

For one, I simply feel more compassion for people, especially addicts, as human beings. The cure for any misunderstanding is, of course, more understanding. The cure for most disagreements is more data—more facts. So, in the process of having the conversations that informed and inspired this book, and learning about the life stories of these people, my opinions on certain controversial topics have changed.

Human beings are messy, and unique, and though some of us may follow similar behavioral patterns, we all arrive where we are through the unique events in our lives and how they shape us. Though it may never be possible to truly understand someone, from top to bottom, it is always worthwhile to try to learn more, to understand more, especially about people who are often misunderstood, or with whom you disagree, or who make radically different life choices than you do.

There is one concept that I found especially edifying: suffering is not the only, necessary cause for creating great art, as many people believe. From the book *Creativity and the Performing Artist: Behind the Mask*:

> Within some performing arts genres, young performers are exposed to alcohol and drugs with the caveat that this usage will enhance creativity and guarantee success. Many pop icons and jazz musicians believe this common misconception. Sadly, this behavior is frequently related to significant decreased life expectancy. Performers such as Jim Morrison, Janis Joplin, and Jimi Hendrix actually lost their motivation to create as their addictions worsened.[308]

This meme still spreads among young people—that you have to subject yourself to some kind of mental torture to

308   *Creativity and Performing Artist: Behind the Mask*, by Paula Thomson and Victoria S Jaque (Academic Press, US: 2017)

be inspired, that all genius is soldered together by tragedy. Neurochemically, this is a misconception, and mental suffering and creativity do not cause each other—they are often caused by a third factor, and so occur together. Correlation does not equal causation. That third, causal factor is, in layman's terms, who you are—meaning, the structure of your brain, your genetics, and environmental triggers for those genetics.

The art and the pain are simply branches of the same tree, and the trunk of that tree is your individual mind. So it seems that the light at the end of the tunnel comes, as much wisdom does, from an old adage your dad probably used to say to you as a kid: Know thyself.

This lesson cannot come too late in the game, as these problems are not simply relics of a bygone era, or features of a particular moment in time, or even unique to a particular musical genre. As this book was being written, yet another top musical artist passed away at right around this first spike on the age graph: Swedish electronic music producer Avicii, at age 28. As of this writing, a statement from the family has led to speculation that his death was a suicide.

Avicii was a talented DJ who transformed the EDM scene with his genre-blending approach to making music. His song, "Levels" became a smash-hit in 2011 and was followed by hits like, "Wake Me Up," and "Hey, Brother," as well as an astonishing tour schedule. His astronomical success and increasingly pop/folk sound caused people to say he had perhaps "sold out." When asked in a 2014 *Rolling Stone* interview "Have you felt like you've been walking the line of being a sellout?" Avicii replied, "No. It's never been my goal to just make more money and be more famous. That's more my manager and his vision of grandness. It has always been about building for the future." [309]

The young man had, apparently, felt some fairly serious mental health trouble on the horizon and taken steps to avoid it. He had struggled with existential crises about (according to his family) "meaning, life, and happiness." In the 2017 documentary, *Avicii: True Stories*, he is seen to suffer from social anxiety and depression. The doc chronicles his path to retirement (at the height of his popularity and demand) at only 26. Heavy drinking and complications from pancreatitis had resulted in at least two hospital stays, shortly after which he would continue to perform even though he would be visibly dazed and almost unable to keep his eyes open. The documentary also shows a fair amount of pressure from fans and those closest to him to continue touring, despite the fact that "he had [...] repeatedly warned that the touring lifestyle was going to kill him, but he was being pressured to continue." [310]

As Neil Jacobson, a Geffen Records executive who worked closely with Avicii put it, "The productions became gigantic and overwhelming [...] He had the duality of having a gigantic sense of theatrical ambition

309   "Avicii on Selling Out and His $1500 Laser Pointer," by Gavin Edwards, RollingStone.com, 02/02/2014.
310   "DJ and Producer Avicii Warned, 'I'm Going To Die' In a Documentary Released 6 Months Before He Was Found Dead At 28," by Allison Millington, BusinessInsider.com, 04/25/2018.

but, at the same time, being a very humble and simple guy. He was caught between the two, and the life began grinding on him." [311]

Avicii is not an outlier: new information is surfacing that EDM DJs, like any other touring act, are suffering from a high frequency of mental health issues, which get brushed aside because of their material wealth:

> Academic studies show that working in the arts can put a strain on the mental health of anyone, whether you're scraping by in a squat or raking in six figure cheques in your Las Vegas penthouse [...] 60% of the musicians surveyed by UK charity Help Musicians said they'd experienced depression [...] Sleep deprivation, isolation on the road and long months away from support networks of family and friends, a competitive and critical circle of peers, internet haters, and a job characterized by both massive highs and crushing lows: it can all work together to make life miserable for even the most successful artist...
>
> Vijaya Manicavasagar is the Director of Psychological Services at the Black Dog Institute, a non-profit established to research and treat mental illness. Manicavasagar told *THUMP* that frenetic touring puts people at particular risk of mental health issues not only because the lack of

311   "Inside Avicii's Final Days," by David Browne, RollingStone.com, 04/27/2018.

sleep and unhealthy lifestyle make it hard to keep "your moods and emotions at an even keel," but also because partying hard can mask people's underlying troubles.

"If they're feeling low or if they're feeling anxious, they might attribute it mistakenly to, 'oh well, I've just been partying very hard, I'm hungover, whatever', so they may not even realize that actually there is an underlying problem here," [312] Manicavasagar said.

Equally, going through the highs and lows of partying constantly can mask the jagged up and down symptoms of bipolar disorder. And often people with anxiety or depression will party even harder to try and feel sociable.

"They look at tried and true ways in the past that might have cheered them up," Manicavasagar said, "but it's probably not such a good idea to be doing that just to mask or compensate for a low mood or an anxiety problem, when actually they need professional help." [313]

So, once again, the best way to inoculate oneself against the troubles that plague our artists is to know oneself. Learn about yourself, to guard against the things, within and outside of your mind, for which you are at risk. If you find a problem, seek out professional

---

312   "Depression, Isolation and Drug Addiction: When DJing Becomes a Mental Health Issue," by Nick Jarvis, THUMP/Vice.com, 07/05/2016.
313   Ibid.

help, without shame or hesitation. To those who, like myself previously, find mental health issues difficult to understand or take seriously from the outside, I would say that knowledge is power, and education is key. Read, and listen, and you will find that you will change your mind about things you never thought you could (like I did). Changing one's mind in the presence of new data is evidence that one's mind is actually in touch with reality. It is a good thing, I think, to change one's mind, if the evidence is compelling enough.

On top of that, to the artists I would add: take care of yourself, so that you can keep making the music, the rock 'n' roll, the blues, the jazz, the paintings, and the work that only you can make.

Acknowledgments

I would like to first extend my thanks to the friends and families of victims of suicide, drug overdose, and mental illness, especially the figures mentioned in this book. I haven't always been as understanding of these issues as I am beginning to be now. The voices trying to explain these issues to those of us who stand outside of them are only recently amplified enough for people like me to hear. I thank you for your patience with the rest of us.

Thank you to the lovely folks at powerHouse Books for being patient, and for allowing us to explore a macabre but fascinating topic.

I would like to thank the powerful Robby Krieger, a celebrated (and, I think, still under-celebrated) songwriter of legendary proportions. Thank you for speaking on a topic I'm sure you're weary of by this point.

Thank you to my son's good friend Phil "Spiky" Meynell, for his firsthand account of his friend Amy Winehouse's personal life. Primary sources are invaluable for a project like this, one that handles a sensitive subject, and they can be hard to come by because the wounds of losing a loved one can stay open a long time.

Thanks to the fascinating and brilliant Dr. James Fallon for distilling the complex science behind this stuff down to layman's terms so we can all, at last, understand it.

Thanks for my son Nick, for helping me edit this book, and for fighting me when I need to be fought.

INDEX

Aberdeen, Washington, 153, 160
addictions, 20, 28-30, 31, 32, 53,
    92, 95, 164, 167, 169, 188,
    254
alcohol, 30, 189, 190, 209, 242, 254
    See also substance abuse; drugs;
    abuse, 26; Buckley, Jeff, 228;
    Cobain, Kurt, 149; Hendrix,
    Jimi, 75, 76; Joplin, Janis, 98;
    McKernan, Ron "Pigpen,"
    205; Morrison, Jim, 108, 114,
    115; Winehouse, Amy, 185,
    186
almost-27s, 212–31; Buckley, Jeff,
    232-37; Buckley, Tim, 228–
    31; Redding, Otis, 221-227
Amy, 178, 181
Andrew, Sam, 92, 95
An Unfinished Life (Gould), 226
anxiety, 155, 241, 256, 258
Are You Experienced (The Jimi Hen-
    drix Experience), 74, 78
The Atlantic, 153
Aubert, Martin, 140
Austin, Texas, 89, 90, 92, 100
Avicii, 255, 256, 257
Avicii: True Stories, 256

Back to Black (Amy Winehouse), 182,
    184, 187, 190
Baez, Joan, 93
Band of Gypsies (Jimi Hendrix), 77
Basquiat, Jean-Michel, 127-145,
    249; birth of, 128; childhood
    of, 128-30; death of, 145;
    drugs, 134, 140, 142, 144; ed-
    ucation of, 129-31; friendship
    with Andy Warhol, 132, 135,
    143, 145
Beatles, The, 68, 207, 223, 226, 245
Beckett, Larry, 231
Bell, Max, 203
Bennett, Karleen, 87
Bennett, Tony, 177, 187, 188

Berg, Amy, 87, 102
Bernstein, Nils, 159
Berry, Chuck, 55, 69
Bey, Yasiin. *See* Mos Def
Big Brother and the Holding Com-
    pany, 92, 95, 100
Blackbourne, Stan, 62
Black Power, 77
Black Sabbath, 48
Blake, William, 109, 111
Blood, Sweat & Tears, 231
Boston University, 201
Bowie, David, 13, 236
brain chemistry, 242, 244, 247
Brandis, Jonathan, 213-217
Brathwaite, Fred, 127, 131
"Break On Through" (the Doors),
    114
*Brian Jones: The Making of the Rolling
    Stones* (Trynka), 59, 62
Brown, James, 222
Brown, Willie, 40
Buckley, Jeff, 229-37; alcohol use,
    234; death of, 235; "Hallelu-
    jah," 236
Buffalo Springfield, 113

Canned Heat, 201, 202, 203, 205,
    223
Can't Buy Me Love (Gould), 226
Caserta, Peggy, 96
Chandler, Chas, 67, 73, 76
Cheltenham, England, 54
Clapton, Eric, 37, 45, 63
Clarksdale, Mississippi, 42
club, origin of, 15-19
Cobain, Frances, 170
Cobain, Kim, 155, 170
Cobain, Kurt, 15, 17, 149-71, 198;
    alcohol, 149; childhood of,
    153-5; death of, 165; depres-
    sion, 163, 167, 168, 171, 173;
    divorce of parents, 156-8;
    drugs, 168, 171, 172, 173;

Nirvana, 152, 153, 154, 159, 166, 172, 236; suicide, 149, 153, 156, 167, 168, 169
Cooke, Sam, 73, 198, 221
Cooper, Alice, 48
Cornell, Chris, 13
Cortez, Diego, 133
Courson, Pamela, 118, 119
creativity, 249, 254
Creativity and the Performing Artist: Behind the Mask (Jaque and Thomson), 254
Cropper, Steve, 224
Crosby, Bing, 109, 222
Crossfire Hurricane, 56, 208
"Cross Road Blues" (Robert Johnson), 45

Davis, Clive, 94
Deadheads, 207, 210. *See also* Grateful Dead
death of celebrities, 14
"demon" persona, 48
Densmore, John, 111, 116-7
depression, 20, 24, 26, 28, 35, 100, 163, 167, 168, 169, 171, 178, 203, 204, 216, 231, 240, 241, 242, 243, 245, 246, 247, 248, 256, 257, 258
Diaz, Al, 129, 131, 163
documentaries: *Amy*, 178, 181, 186; *Avicii: True Stories*, 256; *Crossfire Hurricane*, 56, 208; *Janis Joplin: Little Girl Blue*, 87, 102; *Montage of Heck*, 152, 153, 156, 169; *The Radiant Child*, 131, 139; *The Search for Robert Johnson*, 39; *When You're Strange*, 107
Dodds, Charles, 38
the Doors, 15, 25, 107, 108, 109, 111, 112, 113, 114, 118, 120. *See also* Morrison, Jim; "Break On Through," 114; Ed Sul-

livan Show, 115; "Light My Fire," 108, 112, 114, 144; *The Soft Parade*, 118; "The End," 114; *Waiting For the Sun*, 117
The Doors of Perception (Huxley), 111, 112
"Do You Love Me" (KISS), 150
drugs, 15, 17, 18, 23, 27, 28, 30, 31; Basquiat, Jean-Michel, 134, 140, 142, 144; Cobain, Kurt, 166, 169, 170, 171; the Doors, 113, 138, 121 (*see also* Morrison, Jim); Hendrix, Jimi, 80, 81; Jones, Brian, 56, 58; Joplin, Janis, 91, 92, 95, 96, 99, 100, 102; "sex, drugs, and rock 'n' roll," 23, 47; Winehouse, Amy, 184, 187, 193

Ed Sullivan Show, 115
Edwards, David "Honeyboy," 44

Fab 5 Freddy. *See* Brathwaite, Fred
Fallon, James, 239-51
Father Of The Delta Blues (Son House), 202
Fielder, Jim, 231
Fielder-Civil, Blake, 180, 182, 184, 185, 186, 193
Foo Fighters, 151
Foster, Fred, 98
Fry, Glenn, 13

Garcia, Jerry, 208, 209
genetics, 60, 241, 242, 246, 255
Getz, David, 92
Giles, Jeff, 203
Gould, Jonathan, 226
graffiti artists, 129, 130, 131, 140, 141. *See also* Basquiat, Jean-Michel
Grateful Dead, 201, 207, 208, 209, 210, 223
Grohl, Dave, 151, 152, 158, 168

grunge, 68, 149, 151, 160, 198. *See also* Cobain, Kurt

The Guardian, 181

guitars, 42, 44, 46, 48, 54, 56, 62, 67, 68, 69, 70, 71, 72, 73, 75, 76, 77, 80, 111, 151, 162, 178, 202, 204, 235

"Hallelujah" (Jeff Buckley), 236

"Hard to Handle" (Otis Redding), 223

Harry, Debbie, 131, 133

Hathaway, Donny, 182

Havers, Richard, 42

Hefner, Hugh, 13

"Hellhound on my Trail" (Robert Johnson), 46

Hendrix, Jimi, 15, 67-83, 223, 254; alcohol, 75, 76; in backup band for Sam Cooke, 73; childhood of, 68-71; death of, 79; military career of, 71; at the Monterey Pop Festival, 74, 93; musical education of, 69-71; in Nashville, Tennessee, 71; in New York City, 73; racial statements of, 77; as songwriter, 75; stance on Vietnam War, 78; substance abuse, 80, 81; Woodstock, 77, 81

Herman, Gary, 56

heroin, 27, 29, 198. *See also* drugs; Basquiat, Jean-Michel, 140, 144, 145; Cobain, Kurt, 156, 161, 162, 163, 165, 167, 170; Joplin, Janis, 95, 96, 97, 98, 99, 123; Winehouse, Amy, 184, 185, 186, 188, 192, 193. Brandis, Jonathan, 216; Redding, Otis, 231

hippie movement, 80, 81, 83, 94, 112, 120, 157, 224

Holly, Buddy, 69

Hooker, John Lee, 203, 204, 205

Hooker 'n Heat (Canned Heat), 203

House, Son, 38, 40, 46, 202, 205

Howlin' Wolf, 55, 69

Hurt, Mississippi John, 202

Huxley, Aldous, 111, 112

interview (James Fallon), 241-50

In Utero (Nirvana), 163

Isley Brothers, 73

Jagger, Mick, 53, 62, 63, 82. *See also* Rolling Stones; drug busts, 61; influences of, 55; parting ways with Brian Jones, 57

James, Skip, 202

Janis Joplin: Little Girl Blue, 87, 102. *See also* Joplin, Janis

Jaque, Victoria S., 254

Jeffrey, Michael, 76

Jenkins, Johnny, 221

The Jimi Hendrix Experience, 74, 75, 76, 77

Johnson, Noah, 38

Johnson, Robert, 15, 37-49, 127, 128, 201, 202, 208; "Cross Road Blues," 45; death of, 43-5; "Hellhound on my Trail," 46; improvement on the guitar, 41-2; influences on, 37; playing with Son House, 40; selling your soul to the devil myth, 45-7; "Terraplane Blues," 43

Jones, Brian, 15, 53-63, 74, 99, 107, 109, 119, 208. *See also* Rolling Stones; birth of, 28; death of, 58; drugs, 56, 61; education of, 54; as founder of the Rolling Stones, 54; influences of, 55; legacy of, 59; obituary, 59; parting ways with the Rolling Stones, 57; substance abuse, 56, 58

Joplin, Janis, 15, 74, 82, 87-103, 117, 140, 208, 222, 223, 254; alcohol, 91, 102; childhood of, 89-90; death of, 99; drugs, 91, 92, 95, 96, 99, 100, 102;

encounter with Jim Morrison, 117; in high school, 89, 94; leaving Texas, 90; "Me and Bobby McGee," 98; Monterey Pop Festival, 93, 94; move to Austin, Texas, 99; *Pearl*, 98; "Piece of My Heart," 95; in San Francisco, CA, 90, 91, 92, 93, 100
Joplin, Laura, 101
Joplin, Michael, 88
Judas Priest, 48

Keeling, Richard, 231
King, B.B., 70, 73
KISS, 150, 207
Kornhaber, Spencer, 153
Kozmic Blues, 96
Krieger, Robby, 25, 111, 261
Kristofferson, Kris, 98

LA Woman (the Doors), 119
Lawrence, Sharon, 79
Lead Belly, 87, 164
Led Zeppelin, 48, 63, 93, 223, 233, 235
Lennon, John, 63, 101, 108
"Light My Fire" (the Doors), 108, 112, 114, 118
Little Richard, 55, 73, 221, 223
Love, Courtney, 153, 161, 165, 198

Madonna, 134, 138
Mallouk, Suzanne, 130, 135, 140, 142, 144
Manicavasagar, Vijaya, 257, 258
Manson, Marilyn, 48
Manzarek, Ray, 110, 111, 117, 118
marijuana, 155, 234. *See also* drugs
Mazzoli, Emilio, 134
McCartney, Paul, 13, 74
McCormick, Robert "Mack," 39, 45
McCulloch, Bill, 43
McKernan, Ron "Pigpen," 201, 207-211; alcohol, 209, 210;

death of, 209, 211
"Me and Bobby McGee" (Janis Joplin), 98
Melody Maker, 67
memberships, Soho House, 19-20
Memphis, Tennessee, 38, 39, 235
mental health, 20, 24, 28, 160, 245, 256
Meynell, Phil "Spiky," 190, 261
Miller, Jimmy, 58
The Mirror, 186
Montage of Heck, 152, 153, 156, 165
Monterey Pop Festival: Canned Heat, 202; Davis, Clive, 90; Hendrix, Jimi, 74, 93; Joplin, Janis, 93, 94; Redding, Otis, 223, 224
Morgen, Brett, 152, 153
Morris, Andrew, 190
Morrison, Jim, 82, 107-123, 254; alcohol, 112, 118, 119; childhood of, 109-11; death of, 119; decency rallies against, 116-7; education of, 109-10; encounter with Janis Joplin, 117; influences of, 109, 111; Père Lachaise Cemetery (Paris, France), 120; persona of, 110; substance abuse, 120
Morrison, Van, 113
Mos Def, 180, 183, 189
MTV, 158, 164
Museum of Modern Art (MoMA), 137

Nairne, Eleanor, 130
Nashville, Tennessee, 71
Nevermind (Nirvana), 158
New Music Express, 67
Niehaus, David, 96, 97, 98, 101
Nirvana, 150, 151, 152, 157, 164, 170, 236. *See also* Cobain, Kurt; *Nevermind*, 158; rise of, 152; "Serve the Servants," 163; "Smells Like Teen Spirit," 158; success and, 155-57;

In Utero, 163
Nosei, Annina, 133, 134, 140
notable mentions, 197-217; Brandis, Jonathan, 213-17; McKernan, Ron "Pigpen," 207-11; Wilson, Alan "Blind Owl," 201-05
Novoselic, Krist, 157, 158, 161, 162

O'Brien, Glenn, 132, 152
Odetta, 89
Oedipus complex, 114, 122
Osborne, Buzz, 150, 155, 156
overdoses, 102, 241. *See also* suicide

patterns, 254
Patton, Charley, 406, 202
Pearl (Janis Joplin), 98
Pearson, Barry Lee, 43
Père Lachaise Cemetery (Paris, France), 120
personal decisions, reasons for, 21
Petty, Tom, 13
Pickett, Wilson, 73
"Piece of My Heart" (Janis Joplin), 95
Plant, Robert, 93, 233
pop culture America, 20
Port Arthur, Texas, 88
prefrontal cortex issues, 243
Presley, Elvis, 14, 69, 70, 109, 120,
Prince, 13
psychedelics, 112. *See also* drugs
The Psychopath Inside: A Neuroscientist's Personal Journey into the Dark Side of the Brain (Fallon), 240

Queen, the, 68
Questlove, 189

The Radiant Child, 131, 139
Redding, Otis, 87, 221–27; childhood of, 221; death of, 224; "Hard to Handle," 223; Monterey Pop Festival, 223, 224; "Respect," 223; " (Sittin' on)

The Dock of the Bay," 224; "These Arms Of Mine," 222
"Rehab" (Amy Winehouse), 181, 182, 184, 186
"Respect" (Otis Redding), 223
Richards, Keith, 37, 53, 63; drug busts, 61; influences of, 55
Rohter, Larry, 63
Rolling Stone magazine, 59, 62, 63, 82, 120, 158, 162, 216, 223, 230, 256
Rolling Stones, 15, 48, 53, 54, 55, 63, 115, 222
Ronson, Mark, 184-5
Rothchild, Paul, 99, 114
Rotten, Johnny, 176

SAMO (same old shit), 131, 132, 144
San Francisco, California, 90, 91, 92, 93
Scharr, Herb, 137
Scharr, Lenore, 137
schizophrenia, 121, 241, 246, 248
Schnabel, Julian, 139
Schoenfeld, Eugene, 210
Science of 27, 239–51
The Search for Robert Johnson, 39
Seattle, Washington, 68, 165, 198
self-medicating, 163, 164, 169
"Serve the Servants" (Nirvana), 163
"sex, drugs, and rock 'n' roll," 23, 47
Shymansky, Nick, 179, 182, 183, 185, 188
Sinatra, Frank, 109, 222
"Smells Like Teen Spirit" (Nirvana), 158
Smith, Bessie, 87, 198
The Soft Parade (the Doors), 118
Soho House, 18-9
songs; "Break On Through" (the Doors), 114; "Cross Road Blues" (Robert Johnson), 45; "Do You Love Me" (KISS), 150; "Hallelujah" (Jeff Buck-

ley), 236; "Hard to Handle" (Otis Redding), 223; "Hellbound on my Trail" (Robert Johnson), 46; "Light My Fire" (the Doors), 108, 112, 114, 144; "Me and Bobby McGee" (Janis Joplin), 98; "Piece of My Heart" (Janis Joplin), 95; "Rehab" (Amy Winehouse), 181, 182, 184, 186; "Respect" (Otis Redding), 223; "Serve the Servants" (Nirvana), 163; "Smells Like Teen Spirit" (Nirvana), 158; "Song to the Siren" (Tim Buckley), 230; "Terraplane Blues" (Robert Johnson), 43; "(Sittin' on) The Dock of the Bay" (Otis Redding), 224; "The End" (the Doors), 114; "These Arms Of Mine" (Otis Redding), 222

"Song to the Siren" (Tim Buckley), 230

Stanton, Harry Dean, 13

Starsailor (Tim Buckley), 230

Stewart, Michael, 140, 141

St. John, Powell, 89-90

substance abuse, 18, 22, 30, 242. *See also* drugs; Jones, Brian, 57; Morrison, Jim, 120; Buckley, Jeff, 235

suicide, 18, 20, 63, 241, 246, 255, 261; Brandis, Jonathan, 216; Cobain, Kurt, 149, 153, 156, 167, 168, 169; Wilson, Alan "Blind Owl," 204

The Sun, 186

The Telegraph, 168

"Terraplane Blues" (Robert Johnson), 43

"(Sittin' on) The Dock of the Bay" (Otis Redding), 224

"The End" (the Doors), 114

"These Arms Of Mine" (Otis Redding), 222

Thomson, Paula, 253

Thrall, Pat, 151, 152

Trynka, Paul, 59, 62

Turner, Tina, 73

27 club, 89; almost-27s (*see* almost-27s); Basquiat, Jean-Michel, 127–45; Cobain, Kurt, 149-71; Hendrix, Jimi, 67–83; Johnson, Robert, 37–49; Jones, Brian, 53–63; Joplin, Janis, 87–103; Morrison, Jim, 107–23; notable mentions (*see* notable mentions); origin of, 15-16; Science of 27, 239–51; Winehouse, Amy, 169–89

UCLA film school, 109

Unplugged (MTV), 164

urban myths, 15, 16, 37, 45, 239

Vietnam War (1955-1975), 78

Waiting For the Sun (the Doors), 117

Warhol, Andy, 132, 135, 143, 145

Waters, Muddy, 55, 69, 71, 202

Weir, Bob, 223

Welding, Pete, 44

When You're Strange, 107

Whisky a Go Go (Los Angeles, CA), 113

The Who, 20

Williamson, Sonny Boy, 44

Wilson, Alan "Blind Owl," 201–05

Winehouse, Amy, 15, 169–89; alcohol, 189, 190; *Back to Black*, 182, 184, 187, 189; birth of, 177; childhood of, 178; death of, 189; drugs, 184, 187, 193, 204; influences of, 177; persona of, 176; "Rehab," 181, 182, 184, 186

Winehouse, Mitch, 181

Woodstock (1969), 81, 96, 202

Worthington, Herbie, 79